Why Women Do What They Do.

Kenneth Madu

ISBN: 0692552677
ISBN 13: 9780692552674

1

Kenneth, Manhattan, 2002

The phone next to the bed rang, and Catherine stirred beside me, and her bare leg cocked over my thigh; her knee warm pressed against my groin, and I wasn't in any hurry to answer the phone. I knew who was calling. It was the front desk informing me I had a visitor. After all, I was in the most expensive hotel in Manhattan, with a magnificent view of the whole of New York. What more could I ask for? Not that I had the money for the hotel; it was just one of those days, and I felt like treating myself. I held a diamond between my fingers, letting it catch the morning light from the window. Pieces of stars—that's what diamonds are, the hardest substance on earth. A twenty-eight-carat diamond, just imagine, but a rare diamond with a history of love, lust, and greed. The worst deadly sins were part of its pedigree.

My visitor wanted the diamond, not me? For a woman knows what she wants at any given time and knows how to get it. The phone rang again, and Catherine pushed her knee harder against my groin, sending a shot of desire through me.

"Answer it," she said.

"It's your sister."

"Fuck her."

I have. "Send her up," I told the caller.

Catherine rolled over onto her other side. Her name was Catherine Maria, and she was from Brooklyn in east New York. At twenty-nine, her body was taut, so adorable actually flawless. Her breasts were small and firm with rosy nipples that always looked like they were excited, young, beautiful, and wild. She reminded me of a young lioness cub I saw in Africa—big enough to rip with teeth and claws but who needed a warm stomach to snuggle up to at night; she was everything I wanted in a woman, but again, she still wanted to play the field. I don't know why, but I loved her. I met her on an American Airlines flight going to Oslo, Norway. She was half Norwegian and half black. I saw her cry, saw her smile, knew her fears. I had doubts. But I loved her.

I slipped on a robe and went into the suite's living room. I pulled the door to the hallway corridor open a few inches. I had already opened the drapes and was calling room service for coffee when Simone pushed the door open.

She hadn't changed in the six years since I had last seen her. Neither had I. She still made my blood pound.

Unlike Catherine's thin, hard body, Simone's body was fleshy, padded succulently so a man could get something in his teeth.

She aroused me infinitely more than her sister did, for she stirred up prurient thoughts in me that I never knew existed. She was exciting, but making love to her was provocative and memorable—if you survived the foreplay.

While Catherine was an overgrown kitten, her sister was definitely a full-grown lioness, able to hunt and kill on her own. She was a few years older than me, in her late thirties, a time in a woman's life when she's the sexiest and most desirable, when she's replaced the thin brightness of youth with plush sensuality.

"You look good," she said, stepping in and closing the door behind her. "Rich, successful, not at all the boy I once seduced."

"Life has been good. I have money, health, envy—everything but a good woman. Good ones who will tolerate me are rare."

"You are probably looking in the wrong places."

She stepped onto the balcony; my hotel suite overlooked the whole of Manhattan, a beautiful view. The sunlight glowed through her white dress, outlining her body.

"White's a deceptive color for you to wear," I said.

"I could take the dress off if you prefer."

She knew me. That's the trouble with being a man—women know that we think more with our private parts than with our brains.

She came closer, near enough for me to feel her body heat, to smell the sex in her perfume. Women don't wear perfume to make them smell sweet but rather to stimulate a man's sex drive.

I knew this woman was trouble—she had tried to kill me once—but I guess it was like the fascination some people get playing with deadly snakes: the danger just made it more exciting.

"I missed you, Kenneth," she said.

"You know where I have been. You stayed with your husband."

"You don't understand loyalty. You have never had anyone to be loyal to. My husband took me off the street, away from selling my body for food and drugs when I was younger than my sister."

"He is old enough to be your grandfather. And you have fucked everyone around him, from his lawyer to his friends."

"I have a woman's needs, but I have always been there for him. When he dies, I will cry at his grave. He knows that." "So what does that make you?"

"The conception of women," I said. So I figured she didn't love him; she was just content with his money.

She came closer, pulled open my robe, and held me with her cold fingers. My blood pounded. Her lips brushed mine. My blood ignited, and I felt every temperature in my body rise. I wanted to push her away, but I was weak.

"I missed you," she whispered.

"Hello, sis." Catherine stood in the bedroom doorway, naked.

Simone's eyes came back to me.

Hmm. Simone and Catherine left, bitching at each other about times and places and things that meant nothing to me. But the game just began. Simone would be back; she knew how to please a man until she got what she wanted.

The coffee came. I stood on the balcony and drank my coffee, thinking about the past and about New York, Europe, Amsterdam, Cuba, and Africa. I never thought of life as a struggle, not even when the chips were down and my luck was running out, but I had learned something about myself, something that might sound strange to my friends and family. I have been running scared most of my life. That's why I went for the gold with everything that I ever did. That's why it had always been all or nothing with me.

I had spent my whole life living like there was no tomorrow.

Maybe there wasn't.

2

Kenneth, Overseas

I wasn't always like this: my heart became cold as I grew older. As a kid growing up, I was different. My mum gave birth to me in Roosevelt Hospital in Manhattan, one of the best hospitals ever. And she took me overseas, and that's where I grew up. Life was different growing up in Amsterdam; my mum was a stewardess for British Airlines, and she was making good money.

My mother met my father on a plane to London, and from then on, life changed. My father grew up in England and was an international business man, doing import and export. My father handled business well, with quiet strength. He wasn't the type to get excited or angry during negotiations—he was more cerebral than most of the dealers I have seen in action.

I never had to work a day in my life; my mum just bought a house, had all her kids at twenty-seven—two girls and two boys—put all of us in a house in Europe, and hired four maids to take care of us. I never wanted for anything; everything I wanted I had, and since my mum was a stewardess, she took us everywhere she went, so growing up, my siblings and I had a choice to travel to different countries—Italy, France, Japan, and the Netherlands. It was fun.

My mother was beautiful, with soft black hair, warm brown eyes, and beautiful pearly skin. I inherited her eyes and a black tint to my own black hair. I remember her as quiet and delicate. She never raised her voice, but she commanded the household with the velvet iron of her will. My father never disagreed with her, at least never in my presence, and I never heard him raise his voice to her.

Kids don't really understand the love their parents have for each other. It wasn't until I grew up and loved a woman myself that I understood how much my mother meant to my father. In those days, I really only understood how much she meant to me.

I was confused growing up. My mother kissed a girl, and I was shocked; I thought it was the way of life. Then my mother told me that my father had walked out on me when I was seven weeks old, but he came back because he said he couldn't live without my mother, that there was no him without her, and that she completed him.

My father always treated my mother with an old-fashioned gentleness and respect, almost as if she was something more than a wife to him. Maybe he treated her a little differently because he was a bit older than she was. In my father's quiet, analytical way, I think he intuitively knew that someday he would lose her.

Inside his home office, my father opened an old safe and removed a cigar. He lit it, and then he had me sit on his knee, and he removed a nine-carat diamond. It glistened with light and sparkled, its forty-eight facets turning the white light into sparkling brilliance. A well-cut diamond is so alive with light and color that it appears to be a blaze of glittering fire.

"I met your mum in seventy-seven," my father said. "I was flying to England through British Airlines. And that's when I saw your mum in her stewardess uniform. Look at this diamond, and tell me what you see."

I examined it. "It's flawless," I said.

"Yes, it's flawless; there are no cracks or blemishes, nothing to diminish its beauty. It's like looking into a star; that's what I saw the first time I saw your mother. I looked into her eyes, and I saw her heart and knew that she was the woman I would love for the rest of my life.

"Kenneth," he said, calling me by my first name, "when you marry, always give your wife a flawless diamond so that the marriage will be perfect. My marriage was perfect because the woman I married is a gem without equal." His eyes became watery, and he looked down. He said that when he saw my mother, the earth shook under his feet, and he heard gypsy violins, and time stood still.

Then the pain came: My father lost his job, so my mother took care of all of us, but my father was not satisfied. He felt low, beneath. Then came abuse, cheating, beating, and screaming. Life changed, and my mother became furious about the beating and the abuse. Then she met someone else, and she was happy; she loved my father, and yet she was seeing someone else. I thought I understood the logic, but I never did until I got older, loved a woman, and understood why women do what they do.

My father found out about the other guy and became heated. He found the guy, almost killed him, and told him stay away from my mother. He hit my mother and drove her away, yet he was miserable. He loved her, and I woke up at night hearing him cry out her name.

It made me question his love. I never understood love, but I could see in his eyes that without my mother, he was lost because he started taking out his frustration on us kids. He beat us every day, saying that he was making sure that we were disciplined.

Overseas, beating a child is discipline. And after my mum left, my father knew he needed her; he knew he was finished without her. I grew up understanding the power of a woman and why they do what they do. I also knew my father needed my mother.

My father called out my name. "Kenneth, what do I do?"

I was pretty young, so I was confused, but I knew and understood the concepts of love and betrayal. I told him to go find her, and he did. He brought her home a week later. My mother looked different because she had cried so much. She said her pain was deeper than tears. Her eyes were puffy, and I felt the sensitivity of her skin. Her fingers were cold. I took her hand and stared at the diamond on her finger, the ring my father had given her when they were married. She still had it on. And I cried.

So my aim was to leave and start a new life, do something different. My first encounter with a woman was when I was nine years old. The maid that my mother hired kissed me, and since then, everything has changed. She taught me everything I needed to know about a woman. She was Portuguese, with an exceptional accent and exquisite jet-black hair that I fell in love with. Even though I never knew what love was or meant.

It started one morning when she asked me to help her fix the lightbulb in her room. I followed her into her room.

She showed me a new lightbulb. A glass light cover would have to be removed to change the bulb. She had a wooden stool beneath the light. I started to get on the stool, and she stopped me.

"The stool is too weak for you. You hold the stool, and I'll fix the light."

"Okay…"

I knelt by the stool and held it with both hands. She put her hand on my head to steady herself as she climbed onto the stool. My blood instantly heated from the smell of jasmine and the warmth that radiated from her.

She stood upright on the stool. Her short thin-strapped black dress only came halfway down her thighs, exposing her copper-toned bare legs, which were firm and smooth and shone as if she had nylons on.

When she reached up to fiddle with the little screws that held the glass cover, her short dress went up, and I saw the black panties covering her crotch. I don't know if my hands shook or the stool, but she lost her balance and started falling.

I stood up, grabbing her bare legs. She fell against me and slid down. I kept my hands around her, and she slipped through them. My hands went up her bare legs and into her dress until I had a handful of her breast in each hand by the time her feet hit the floor. She looked up at me with her mysterious eyes barely open. Her little breasts were pressed against my chest. She said something, but I wasn't sure what.

My hands were burning; my brain was frying. The smell of her jasmine perfume stole my mind. I squeezed her breasts. She stood on tiptoe and pulled my head down with her hands. Her lips were hot and wet and tasted like sex as she pushed her tongue into my mouth.

When she pulled back, I was breathless and just stared at her. I was hard and ready to burst. A shoulder strap had slipped down, and her breast was exposed. I felt its sexual message down to my toes. She smiled and kissed me again with her wet lips as she pulled down the other shoulder strap. I put my hand on the exposed breast, but she pulled it away and led my head down to it. I kissed her breast and tasted her nipple with my tongue.

I was shaky and scared and needed to release. My dick pressed against my pants so hard it hurt.

Suddenly, her hand went down inside my pants, and she grabbed my penis.

"No!" I cried. I leaned against her as I came on her hands.

"It's okay," she whispered. "Boys can cum many times."

She led me into the bedroom and to her bed. She quickly pulled her dress over her head and stood before me, breasts naked, wearing only bikini panties. I fumbled off my clothes, all except my underwear. I was a cherry. I was as nervous as hell and had already preejaculated.

She came and put her arms around me and rubbed her naked breasts against my chest, then pulled down my shorts. I stepped out of them and tried to steer her onto the bed, but she slipped from my grasp and pushed me down onto the bed on my back. Working at the top of my head, she started kissing me, licking my neck, and going down to each nipple. I thought breast fucking was only something guys did to girls, but I was wrong. When her erotic tongue teased my nipple, I felt it down to my toes.

Her tongue continued down my stomach to my penis, which was still limp. She held it up and kissed underneath it, running her tongue over my testicles and sucking my balls.

Then she came up and put my whole penis in her mouth. As she sucked on my penis, it started to stiffen and get bigger. Her mouth slipped off my erection, and she grinned at me.

She slipped off her panties. I tried to pull her down and mount her, like I had once seen a guy do with a girl in the back seat of a car at a drive -in, but she pushed me back down and straddled me, kissing me as she rubbed herself against my hard-on. She was soft and wet, and I slipped in easily and started pumping, and I gasped as her strong legs tightened their grip on me. It was heaven. This was the dream.

I stopped going to school. Since my mother was always flying, she was barely home; she just kept sending us postcards from different countries. So instead of going to school, I stayed with the maid, whose name was Kathy.

She was a twenty-four-year-old woman who knew what she was doing, and she told me she wanted me. I never knew what she was doing, but all she did was kiss me and make me do things to her. She told me when to stop, how to touch her, and what things to do to her, and this happened over and over again till I was fifteen years old.

She told me she was teaching me how to love a woman. For seven years, Kathy did things to me and had me do things to her. I mean, I woke up one morning, and she was naked in front of me, and for two hours straight, we did things to each other. I became so good at what I did that I thought I loved her.

She was all I knew. I knew every part of her body with my eyes closed; I had kissed every part of her, and she taught me all I knew; I knew her innermost thoughts.

Kathy taught me more about sex in a month than people learn in a lifetime. She was a sex animal.

"Kenneth, all men are impatient," she told me as I jumped on her naked bones. She pushed me to the side. "You have to talk to a woman with your hands and lips before you pump her."

She had me start at the top of her head and come down the sides of her cheeks. My lips caressed the soft skin of her neck and under her ear and down the lush valley between her breasts. I ran my tongue over her nipples, slipped down to tease her belly button with my tongue, and worked my way down the insides of her thighs and to the soles of her feet before my head disappeared into the pink between her legs. She taught me to lick her vulva and go back to her lips so she could taste her own femininity before I slowly returned to the pink and the little button there.

"Work it slow," she told me, moaning with pleasure as I wetly kissed her neck while my penis spoke to her womanhood.

After a while, I knew I was good because this happened for seven years straight.

"You're very good," she said

On the day I turned fifteen years old, my mother flew in to try to surprise me. I never knew she was coming, and she walked in on Kathy in my room kissing me. My mother became so furious; I had never seen my mother that mad. She beat Kathy with every bone inside her while screaming, "How dare you kiss my baby! You slut. You whore."

But the damage was already done because Kathy had done more than kiss me. My mother fired her, and I cried, thinking I was in love. So, I lost Kathy. I never saw her again.

There was something else stunning I discovered about myself as I grew older. I had no real friends—no college pals, no business contacts. It never occurred to me until now that I was loner.

There had been a lot of women in and out of my life, but no one that stuck. I had a girl named Carlotta, but she was on a different planet than I was. What I had was a bunch of acquaintances but no real friends. I didn't have a running buddy; there was no one to back me up if I had trouble coming front and back.

I told my mother I was going to New York and that I was taking my sisters with me. She said no and asked me why New York.

"It's America, and America is the one country in the world where a foreign accent does not mean you're a foreigner," I said.

She said okay and told me that my sisters would come after me. She said she had called a friend of hers to pick me up from the airport and told me to be a good boy. She said, "No more allowance every week."

I said, "Mum, please, I need it." I had never worked a day in my life, and I never knew what it was to be broke. "Mum, I don't know what a job is," I said

She said, "Learn, my son."

I was seventeen years old with so many memories. I'd been to at least fifteen countries, I spoke four languages, and I had lived in Egypt, Nigeria, Italy, France, Brazil, Germany, and England.

But I grew up in Amsterdam, Netherlands, where life was beautiful. I saw so many things growing up, where drugs, prostitution, and drinking were legal professions.

Everything was just a way of life,

I saw everything you could possible think of. Since my mother was a flight attendant, I had the opportunity to travel overseas and see different countries and see things in a different aspect of life.

I have two sisters, Penny Lope and Jennifer, and a brother named Tobi. My sisters went to school in England, and my brother was in Africa. So, life was beautiful. Of course, there were bad times, but in general, life was okay before I left for New York.

My mother gave me an American Express credit card, and I left like there was no tomorrow.

3

Kenneth, New York, 2005

I went alone to AMS, Amsterdam-Netherlands Airport and took a taxi to the terminal that KLM-Royal Dutch Airlines flew out of. Nobody had volunteered to see me off, and I had asked no one. The only way to start a new life is to leave the old one behind.

I felt funny in the taxi and leaned back, trying to figure out what was wrong. Surprisingly, for a guy who had never worked a day in his life. Something else was bothering me. I found it easy to give things up. Nothing was permanent.

I was going through airport security when I saw a woman who was about my age, or maybe a couple of years older, passing through the metal detector ahead of me. I liked the view from the back, and it got even better when I saw the rest of her. She had this long jet-black hair like my mother's, one of my many weakness.

A book had slipped out of her open bag as it went through the security scanner. I grabbed it and called after her as she was walking away. "You dropped this." I looked at the title. "*The Social Economics of Children in Africa.* I think I saw the movie," I said, grinning and handing her the book.

She gave me a look that could kill in an instant. "Did you enjoy the part where children are cannibalized for food?"

Oh, shit. She was that kind—idealistic and out to save the world.

She joined a group of three men and another woman heading down the concourse. If it hadn't been for the put-down, I probably wouldn't have given her another thought. She was attractive but definitely subzero. I'm not one of those men who grovels at the feet of women who step on them, but it always makes the chase more interesting when there are hurdles to jump. Besides, there was the exquisite jet-black hair.

I got behind the group at the gate's check-in desk. When it was my turn with the young Portuguese woman behind the counter, I indicated the girl with jet-black hair across the room.

"I want her bumped up to first class, to the seat next to mine. I don't care what it costs." I still had my American Express card that my mum had given me. I couldn't have left home without it.

"Is that your wife?"

"Not yet."

"What's her name?"

"You will have to tell me."

The woman gave me an appraising look. "Your Portuguese is very good, Mr. Kenneth."

"My mother is Portuguese."

"We have rules about these things."

"Americans have rules about these things. Foreign guys like me have too much soul to let a technicality stand in the way of romance."

"Why don't you just ask her yourself?"

"I tried to put the make on her with my usual charm and wit and stuck my foot in my mouth. She is a very serious woman with world-shattering matters on her mind."

"And you..."

"I have a completely one-track mind.'

The woman signed. "Yes, you certainly have Portuguese blood in your veins." She gave the girl with jet-black hair a look and checked her computer. "Andeshia Bailey, Dr. Andeshia Bailey. She is ticketed with a UN group."

"How do I get her seated by me?"

"What are your intentions with Dr. Andeshia?"

"To make love with her when we reach New York."

She nodded. "Well, that's certainly nothing the airline would object to, as long as you wait until you leave. The seat next to you is open. *Boa sorte!*"

I barely acknowledged Dr. Andeshia as she hesitated in the plane aisle, looking at her boarding pass. Still appearing preoccupied, I got up so she could take the window seat. I didn't want to show too much interest at first. It's better to let an ice princess make the first move. We were airborne and had been served drinks before she spoke to me.

"I have never flown first class before. Thank you."

I shrugged. "You can't trust anyone with a secret nowadays. Did she tell you why I wanted to sit next to you?"

"She said you planned to seduce me."

"And?"

"I took the upgrade, but only for a better meal and a comfortable seat, Mr. Kenneth."

"If you knew me better—"

"Mr. Kenneth, may I call you K?"

"Mister is fine."

"Mister, you are irrelevant."

"Christ, I have been called plenty of things, but what the hell is irrelevant? It sounds like a social disease. Andeshia, did your mother pack you on her back during the Berkeley demonstration in the sixties when you were a baby?"

"Is that how you view concern for world suffering? As a throwback to the sixties? You are the most completely uninformed individual, outside your own selfish pleasures, I have ever encountered."

"I will change; I promise."

"Mr. Kenneth, do you know what I like about you?"

"Nothing, absolutely nothing."

"Now that we have that out the way, will you have dinner with me in New York?"

"I'd rather eat with a viper."

"Is that a yes?"

4

New York

As we came out of customs and into the main concourse, I made one last try with Andeshia.

"Are you sure you won't have dinner with me?" I asked.

"In all honesty, I should buy you dinner for the verbal assault you put up with for thousands of miles. But I'm going to be very busy in New York—meetings every day, and dinners every night—so I'm afraid I'm going to have to pass on repaying you."

"Too bad; I'm going to be awfully lonely here in New York, not knowing a soul."

"Oh, I don't think you are going to be lonely." She nodded over my shoulder. A woman was holding up a handkerchief with *Kenneth* written on it in lipstick. She laughed and waved the handkerchief when she saw me staring.

"Good hunting," Andeshia said, walking away.

"I'm Chandler's wife; your mum told me to pick you up. Simone told me. Sorry about the handkerchief, but other than your age and sex, I didn't know who to look for."

She spoke English with an intriguing accent. Simone drove a pearl-white vintage Bentley. It was a little too tame and conservative for my taste in transportation, but she looked good in it.

She radiated naked sensuality. Her black hair, green eyes, and pale skin, which was almost as pearly as the car, accentuated the diamonds she wore—they were big ones—on her ears, around her neck, and on her wrists and fingers. They all had unique settings, but she wore no other gems except diamonds. That was unusual. Most women mixed their jewels, adding some rubies or sapphires for color. Although I noticed her choker had several yellow and green diamonds and even a rare light-pink diamond. While the colors looked good, I knew they were not the best-grade diamonds. The choker would have been worth a fortune if the colored diamonds had been flawless rather than the sort of thing you wore to pick someone up at the airport.

Rather than appearing ostentatious, the jewels looked good on her, like a diamond collar around the neck of a sleek jungle cat.

I did a quick calculation of the age difference between her and her husband, who had to be about my father's age, which would make him in his late sixties or early seventies. He was about twice Simone's age, which I guessed to be around thirty-four.

A hot young woman and a rich old man—probably not a match made in heaven, but I hadn't seen Chandler, her husband, yet.

Something didn't strike me right about Simone. She had an edge to her. It wasn't so much the hard veneer some woman get who have been treated roughly and have had to fight to survive. I saw a little of that in Andeshia, a don't-tread-on-me attitude. Simone's demeanor was quieter and more subtle but infinitely more threatening. While Andeshia might be tempted to scratch my eyes out, I suspected Simone was capable of kicking me in the balls and putting a knife at my throat if I pissed her off.

I saw the first sign of it when we stepped out of the terminal. She had illegally parked the Bentley in front of the terminal—the arrogance of the rich. A traffic cop with an attitude written on his face was waiting, but he didn't get three words out of his mouth before she gave him a verbal tongue-lashing. I didn't know a lot of Spanish street slang, but I got the idea that her words weren't the sort of talk New York traffic cops often hear from women driving Bentleys.

"*Bastardo*," she said as we pulled away from the curve. "Petty little people with petty little rules."

"Remind me not to try to enforce any of my rules on you."

She laughed. "I'm sorry, but I don't like policemen." She laughed again. "I usually don't launch such attacks on them. This one must have reminded me of someone I ran into when I was a girl."

It made me wonder what kind of past life she had led that had brought her into conflict with cops. And whether her present still offered the opportunity.

"You must think I'm horrible."

"No, actually, I need to improve my Spanish vocabulary, and I just learned some new words. I'm just not sure what sort of people I can use it on."

She laughed again. She laughed easily and freely, without reserve, just as she grew anger quickly and without restraint. I found myself immediately attracted to her sexually. Unlike Andeshia, who made a man give chase, no doubt from some sort of primeval instinct. Maybe so, but there's also another kind of woman a man is irresistibly attracted to; it's the same sort of attraction a moth has when batting its wings on the edge of a volcano. Women like Sharon Stone in *Basic Instincts* and Julia Roberts in *Pretty Woman.* Some bad men have the fatal magnetism too, attracting good women to themselves.

I told myself to keep my zipper pulled up tight. From what I'd heard about Chandler, her husband, he was tough not just in business sense but also in a lethal way.

"I'm surprised your father never brought you to New York," she said. "He and my husband did business together long before you were born. I can set you up with her," Simone said.

"With who?"

"The girl with jet-black hair you were trying to hustle as you got off the plane."

"Do you run a dating service?"

"No, I noticed she was wearing a UN badge. She and her colleagues are here to meet with Portugal's Aid Society."

"You know someone with the society?"

"Intimately. I'm the chairwoman."

Finding out Simone headed a charitable relief organization was no more surprising than if she had said she was an astronaut, not that there was a contradiction about a sensual animal being the chairwoman of an African relief society. But Simone didn't seem like the charitable sort or a pillar of high society.

She laughed at the look on my face. "Chandler has a special interest in the African Relief Society."

Simone indicated the scenery we were passing. It was all concrete buildings and freeway from the airport, but New York is beautiful. Manhattan, where we live, is thirty minutes from Queens, but it is a different world.

"Any children?"

"You will meet Catherine later, my seventeen-year-old daughter. If and when she decides to come home." Simone laughed again.

"Why's that funny?"

"You will have to be careful."

"Do I look like someone who would take advantage of a kid?"

"I wasn't worried about you taking advantage of her."

The drive from JFK took about forty minutes; we drove farther up the road and passed an elegant hotel.

"Once the home of nobility, and now it's a hotel. We are almost to Chandler's house, which is quite lovely too."

Chandler's house. That was an odd way for a wife to refer to the place she shared with her husband. Their relationship was sounding more like a marriage of convenience, as had struck me the first time I saw her. A rich old man with a young trophy wife to keep his feet warm at night. The good life.

We turned on to Fifth Avenue in Manhattan and then turned into an open gateway and drove down a long driveway lined with regal Italian cypresses. The light-gray stone house at the end of the driveway was poised at a walled cliff with a magnificent view of the whole of New York.

It didn't smell of money; it stank of it.

Chandler was waiting for us by a swimming pool that was elevated so that a swimmer could have a view of the ocean through a glass partition.

Chandler had a complexion of polished bronze, silken white hair, and luxuriously thick white eyebrows. A casual dresser, he was slender; his was skin was firm, pulled tight across his facial bones so that it was almost wrinkle-free; and his exposed muscles were hard and thick. Obviously, he was a guy who took care of himself. He was a perfect specimen of a man in his golden years, except for the wheelchair. I wasn't expecting that.

"Shot in the back a couple years ago while playing cards," he said. The portable bar on the patio had a dozen bottles of wine. I sipped a glass of *vinho tinto*, red wine, as I listened. And I studied my father's old friend.

Nothing about Chandler was consistent. He was married to a woman half his age, and he was a hostage to a wheelchair. The house he lived in was a genuine antique, a fabulous place, but the swimming pool beside us was ultramodern, gray bottomed with lots of gilt running through it, and large imperial columns separated the pool patio from the ocean view.

I expected caviar and champagne from the ambiance of the house. Even the wine was a surprise; it was a good inexpensive red table wine, what the Portuguese called *vinho tinto de mesa.*

Simone kissed Chandler when we arrived. Now she sat quietly as he spoke, the good wife.

Chandler had a low, liquid voice, like a fine aged wine. It was the kind of voice that massaged you and made you feel comfortable, but I didn't get sucked into it.

"Men are controlled either by money or a woman. Most can't pass up either."

As the three of us were talking—Chandler, Simone, and I—we heard youthful voices, and several teenage girls came out onto the patio. They were wearing G-strings and bare skin for bathing suits. It wasn't hard to figure out which one was Chandler and Simone's daughter, Tracy. She had Simone's sensuous looks, but she was younger and skinnier.

"Catherine, come over here. I want you to meet someone," Simone said.

The kid sauntered over, full of a sexy seventeen-year-old's conceit and arrogance.

"This is Kenneth, better known as Malcolm," Chandler said. "You have heard me speak of him. His father was an old friend."

She gave me a look up and down. Rude.

"She should be disciplined more, but my husband spoils her and permits her every excess."

"She is not half as wild and crazy as her mother was at her age," Chandler said.

That was an interesting remark. With their age difference, I wondered where Chandler had found his wife. Was it on a school ground?

5

Simone showed me a room with a view of the ocean. I couldn't have done better if I had stayed at the hotel. The room was luxury class, very sophisticated.

"There is a minibar in case you get thirsty, and the buzzer to call the servant is on the end table. We want you to feel at home here. The servant will provide you with anything you want." She paused at the door. "Would you like me arrange dinner with her?"

"With your daughter? She is a little young…"

"With the woman from the airport."

"I did appreciate getting her phone number."

"Why don't I arrange it so that she believes she is meeting an important contributor to the cause of world suffering?"

I laughed. "She already believes that, but I know what you mean. Do you think she'll turn me down if I call?"

"What do you think?"

"It's easy to say no over the phone."

"Yes, and I saw her at the airport. She looks like the dedicated type, a person who fights for truth and justice, not at all the type to waste her time with a man who loves women and fast cars."

"You are a smart woman, Simone. Arrange it for me."

"She is not like us, is she?"

I stood by the window and wondered what she meant.

My conscience soothed, I started to unpack. I heard someone at the door and turned. Simone had left without closing it.

Catherine and one of her G-stringed girlfriends were in the doorway; Catherine leaned over and kissed the girl on the mouth and smiled at me.

"Want to have us?"

"Come back when you grow up."

I slammed the door. I was no fool. Or maybe I was.

I needed a cold shower.

My first encounter with love was very simple; I never knew what love was. And I came to understand that women can be very conniving and heartless when they want to be. It's just in their nature. A woman could look you in the eyes and say she loved you while she fucked your best friend behind your back. I came to the realization that when a woman is tired of you, or the love she had died, or she becomes unhappy, she is capable of doing anything, not to hurt you but to certify her own self.

It's very simple logic: the motive that drives a woman to do what she does is within her. It's logic that simplifies her needs. Once a woman is unhappy at home or you are not giving her what she wants—whether it's sex, money, romance, or stability—and a different guy offers her these things and make her happy in the process, the odds of her cheating or leaving are very high. After doing my research and being in different relationships in twenty countries, I came to understand the most common things in any relationship anywhere in the world are cheating and self-pity, So I know now that a woman could cheat on her man in a heartbeat and be very good at it. There is always a moment when she wonders whether she should give into it or resist. Now, if she is happy and wants to save her relationship, she might; if not, she will. A man only does what a woman allows him to do. But the analogy here is to always be two steps ahead of any woman you are with, always be like the water, always reinvent yourself, always come up with something new every day; if you don't, she'll become bored and lonely. It's like being in a relationship and still feeling alone. Then there is a problem. She is likely to do anything. A bored woman or a lonely woman is likely to cheat in a heartbeat to justify her action, which is to feel wanted.

After experiencing a whole lot about women, I came to understand the simple logic. My friend invited me to his house for dinner. He said, "Ken, watch this. What you know about cooking for your woman, making her dinner, paying her rent, giving her good love, and buying her clothes, which is the number mistake. For if you start buying her clothes and doing all this for her, that's all she will ever know. So once you stop buying things or stop doing things for her, she'll become tired of you, and then boredom will kick in. Or what if you lose your job, and now you can't give her the lifestyle that she is accustomed to? Someone else will, for she'll know you can't provide all the things you used to buy for her. The damage is done, and she loses interest."

So, I was in my friend's house, and he was cooking, sweating, and trying to make a phenomenal meal while his girl was in the living room talking to me. Point blank, if you start off with a woman like that, with you in the kitchen, you'll become the kitchen while she sits and talks to me. You can't start a relationship with you cooking in the kitchen because very soon, you become the kitchen. It won't work.

My friend isn't still with his girl. Is she dating someone else? Yes. The logic is that you have to cripple fear and be truthful with yourself; you don't have to lie or impress her. Don't tell her anything about yourself that you don't want her to know about you. It's that simple. It doesn't matter who you are or what you do; a woman will always leave you if she is unhappy. A happy woman makes a happy life.

It's just the way of life because women are always looking for something new. It's like being in a relationship and still being alone. Women are as devious as men when they want to be. Even though women are beautiful creatures, when a woman becomes bored and lonely, there is nothing she won't do to find happiness or someone who will give it to her.

After a while, the unhappiness becomes so unbearable that she starts cheating or doing anything else to satisfy her own needs.

Once she is unhappy at home and she starts being bored at home, then loneliness kicks in. And someone she meets offers her more. The chances of her cheating are high to satisfy her own needs. But a woman would not cheat on you or disrespect you if she knew you were the center of her world. But if she is still feels alone and bored and unhappy, then she will. A fact? It's only a matter of time.

So, I met my godmother in a restaurant called Slate Plus in Manhattan on Twenty-Third Street and Sixth Avenue. She was at a table waiting for me.

"Mama," I said. And I kissed her hand before sitting down.

"Malcolm, you are so gallant. You would be surprised at how few men in this world today know how to treat a lady."

"I would not. But perhaps you would be surprised by how few women in this world know how to be ladies."

"Like you, I'm not surprised, but I'm dismayed."

We chatted for a moment like two old friends, the gracious older woman and the businessman. I told my godmother that I had a problem finding or getting women who satisfied my particular need, that the average woman bored me, that I had no time for the niceties of romance and lovemaking, and that I was drawn to women from a different world, women with a dangerous edge.

"I have a beautiful girl for you," my godmother said.

"If she is anything like you, she will be special."

My godmother smiled, obviously pleased, even though at her age, she knew it was an empty compliment.

"What makes her special? There are many beautiful women in New York that I could have if I want."

"She is attractive, though I would not call her beautiful. And her body is flawless. But you're right, a man with your looks can certainly have his choice of women. What makes her special, you ask. Have you ever watched a beauty contest? When I see all those beautiful women lined up, I am reminded of the time I went to a horse show and the breeders lined up the thoroughbreds. As your eyes move down the line, sometimes there is something special about a horse that causes you to pause. A look about the horse, the way it holds its head, or the way it paws the ground tells you it is a champion. That is how I think of this woman—put her in a beauty contest, and she might not win the prize, but your eye would pause once you saw her."

"What is this special quality?" I asked

"I can't say exactly, but she has spirit, perhaps even fire. But you have to decide. She gave me the key to her house. She is waiting."

I am a very cautious man; I went to my godmother's house, and she was there, laying on the bed, reading a book. She got up as I walked in.

My godmother was right; she was an attractive woman with the potential to be beautiful, but there was something about her sex appeal that was intriguing. And that something that my godmother had been talking about was special about her. Defiance was my first impression. A young woman who had been kicked and beaten by life, through loneliness, homelessness, and rape. But like the champion she was, she had gotten back on her feet and fought.

As I looked at her, my eyes took on a hardness.

I said, "I'm Ken. And from today, I want you to be my woman."

She spit on my face.

I grabbed her and shoved her toward a wall. "I like a woman with spirit. But you must understand that there are limits to my patience."

I kissed her mouth. She accepted my lips without responding.

I brought out a knife, letting it catch the light and reflect in her eyes, and I brought it down toward her breast. Since I held her toward the wall, her shirt was ajar, leaving her exposed, and she had no bra on.

The knife was so sharp that before I knew it, I had given her a little cut on her breast, causing blood to stream down her skin. "That's my mark. From now on, you are my woman."

I stepped back and put the knife away. I sat down on the edge of the bed to take my shoes off.

I saw it coming, but she was too fast for me. The sharp edge of an ashtray caught me on the side of my neck, leaving a gash and causing me to bleed.

"That's my mark," Tracy said.

6

New York

Simone set up a dinner date for me and Andeshia. The restaurant where I was to meet Andeshia was on Forty-Second and Eighth Avenue and was called “Dave and Buster. Andeshia was waiting in the restaurant’s reception area when I came in. She had her back to me.

“*Ola, fala ingles* (hello, do you speak English)?” I asked in Spanish.

She stared at me, and her lips parted in surprise. Then she shut her mouth and pursed her lips as she blushed. She realized she had been tricked and was deciding between going along with the game or walking out.

“*Non. Parlez-vous francais?*” she asked.

“*Qui,* I speak French. As a matter of fact, I have French families, but let’s stick with English; it’s much easier.”

“I’m supposed to be meeting a very important executive who can help with the aid program. I’m very angry at—”

“No, you are not. I forced Simone to set you up. I told her I had fallen hopelessly in love with you on the plane and that I’d cut myself if I didn’t get to see you. She saved my life.”

"If there's a choice, I'd prefer you cut yourself rather than have dinner with you."

I grabbed both her arms and brought her in close to myself. "Now, we can be civilized and be adult about this thing, or I can embarrass you in this restaurant with loud and vulgar accusations about how you came up to me in the street asking me to pay you for sex."

"You are incorrigible. What do you consider being civilized and adult?"

"We have dinner, make love, have breakfast, make love, and so on."

"You have a one-track mind."

"That's not true. I sometimes think of other exciting things besides making love to a beautiful woman."

She laughed. "Okay, flattery will at least get you dinner. No one's called me beautiful since I was twelve years old. But I'm buying; this way, you won't think you are entitled to dessert because you bought a girl an expensive meal."

"Deal."

After we were given our seats and the menus were brought, she ordered, and then I did. Then she looked at me. "You have to explain something to me. Why have you bothered pursuing me? I'm not beautiful, not sexy, and definitely not attractive. I am a boring administrator and soon will be a field worker for a geology cause. You have your choice of beautiful women who turn your head when you follow them to restaurants. So, what is it, Ken? Was when I turned you down on the plane the first time that had happened in your entire life? Has it traumatized you that a woman could actually not jump into bed with you the moment she saw you?"

"Do you know what I believe in?"

"Tell me."

"Nothing. Absolutely nothing. I have been raised in two religions, and the most significant thing I've gotten from them is the vague threat that I have to be good or God will punish me. I don't give a damn about politics, religion, humanitarianism, sex education, economics, abortions, earthquakes, plane crashes, geology, or anything else that doesn't affect me personally. Maybe that's what intrigues me about you. I'm curious about people like you who believe in a cause and devote their lives for it."

"Do you believe in love?"

"I guess I will just deal with love when I find it."

"How about all your women?"

"Easy come…easy go. Now, enough about me; tell me about you. Why are you such an intellectual soul instead of a doctor or a lawyer?"

"Are you patronizing me? First I am beautiful, and now I'm intellectual."

"So, what makes you tick?"

"This may come as a shock to you, but I wanted a career that gave me a sense of discipline and accomplishment. Knowing that I will spend my days making life easier for people who have been left behind by the modern world."

"Listen to me. I have never worked a day in my life. I am a spendthrift; I waste and throw away vast amounts of money. I deserve some credit for the fact that I have never made a dollar in my entire life. I swear I have never worked at anything long enough or hard enough to screw anyone."

She shook her head. "Why do I get the impression that you're telling the truth and are proud of it? Has it occurred to you that you are wasting your life? How can you be proud of having done nothing?"

"I expect my reward to come in heaven."

She choked on her wine.

"I think we are absolutely compatible. Opposites attract. You are an idealistic woman, and I am just a regular guy." I leaned closer until my lips almost brushed hers. Her warm sensuality radiated.

The moment I saw Simone, I wanted to fuck her. Andeshia was a woman I wanted to make love to.

"Ken..."

"Let's..."

"No. And not because I don't want to." She pushed me back a little and straightened my collar. "I want to very much."

"Do you have someone to account to?"

"Yes, myself. I'm not a strong person. I can't let myself get involved with a man. I won't be able to function if I do."

I was talking about making love, not involvement.

She read my mind. "I'm not like you. Dinner was good, and the company was terrific, but I can't just get involved with you. I can't explain it."

She got up, and I pulled her toward me and hugged her. I said, "I want to be with you."

She pulled away. "It just can't be."

I was just as puzzled about my feelings for her as she apparently was about me.

I was coming out of Forty-Second Street when I ran into Catherine and her friends arguing with some guys. She looked pissed. There were around ten of them, and the kids looked like Catherine—spoiled, rich, and purposeless, with no ambition whatsoever. The four older guys had a harder look about them, especially the one arguing with Catherine.

It wasn't my business, and I kept walking, but I couldn't see the kid get hurt. As I came closer, I realized that she was pissed about ecstasy he had sold her; it wasn't the real stuff.

"Hi, Catherine. Need a ride home?"

The look on her face was that of a girl contemplating whether she should go with me or not.

"Fuck off, *puta*." The guy didn't call Catherine a whore—he used the word on me.

"Let's go—" As I spoke to Catherine and reached for her arm, I spun around, swinging fast and hard, and threw a right across the guy's face. I put my all into that punch, as if my life depended on it. The punch connected great, and the guy fell backward, spitting out blood.

I grabbed Catherine's hands and began to run for my car.

"I didn't need your help, and now you have to pay me for the bad pills."

"Forget it; I am not into buying drugs."

"What are you into? Sex? We can go to a hotel or fuck when we get home."

"Don't you think your parents might be a little put out if they find us having sex in the living room?"

She shrugged. "I learned everything I know about sex from watching my mother."

We got into my car, and I hit the door lock. As I started the engine, she was all over me. She stuck her tongue in my mouth and put my hands on the warm patch between her legs.

She bit my ear. "We can do it here."

I pushed her off and got the car into drive. We were getting out of there.

I slammed the car into drive and took off.

She snuggled close to me. "I like you."

"I'm a guest in your house. Fucking you wouldn't be polite."

"Listen my dad picked Simone up off the street—or maybe from a whorehouse. He's not even my father; she got knocked up by the man who teaches me tennis."

I didn't say anything. Catherine wouldn't be the first kid to hate a parent; hell, some kids even despise their parents. But I wanted information from her, not sex.

"You want me to tell you about my father's plan, don't you?"

"You're into mind reading."

"You are just too honest. I could see the conflict on your face. Do you ask the kid to betray her father or—"

"You said he wasn't your father."

"I don't know who he is, and I don't know what he is up to."

"You're a seventeen-year-old girl; don't you ever call your parents Mum and Dad?"

"They are not my parents. I was found floating in a river in a basket. My mother was a princess who got pregnant before she got married."

"Now I understand you." I understood Catherine was a kid who hated her parents, and she was going to be like that for the rest of her life.

7

I parked the car in the garage. I got out the car, and she got out, came toward me, put her hands around my neck, and kissed me on the mouth. Her body pressed against mine.

"Good evening." It was Simone, Catherine's mother. I tried to break the kiss, but Catherine hung on deliberately.

"Spying?" Catherine asked, letting me go.

"Of course not, Sweetie; I was just worried."

"As you can see, Ken got me home safely."

"I wasn't worried about you. Ken is in a strange country, and there is so much danger here in the city."

Catherine went into the house.

Simone looked at me. "We can talk in the morning." Those were good-night words, but she wasn't moving. "I'm sorry if Catherine was a bother. It's hard nowadays for a kid. I grew up with nothing, not even love. But that made me cherish everything I got. Catherine gets everything free, and she appreciates nothing."

I could feel Simone's heat. The woman had a natural sensuality that radiated sex. I noticed the way her clothes clung to her lush body, the way she walked in a room, her full-shaped lips, and the way her skirt clung to her thighs. There weren't many women in my life that turned me on so fast. But Simone had something extra, a hint of danger. "Something? Well, it's getting late."

She looked at me. "How would you like to die?'

I grinned. "If I have a choice in the matter, I'd rather die in bed and choose the woman whose arms I'm in."

8

The night was warm, with a soft breeze. I pulled open the window and took a hot shower. I turned off the lights and lay naked in bed, enjoying the gentle evening breeze on my body.

An hour had passed when I heard a knock on my door. I'd known she would come. I couldn't deny it; I wanted her.

She dropped her silk robe at the edge of the bed and crawled on top of me. Her breast were strong and full, her nipples rock hard. I leaned up and sucked each succulent nipple. They smelled of rose bathwater. She got my cock between her legs. I was already hard, pushing against her pubis, ready to enter her.

"Were you expecting Catherine?" she whispered.

"I was expecting a woman."

I pulled her to me and kissed her hungrily.

She started down my body, teasing my nipples, and sending goose bumps up my spine. She moved her tongue down my hard body, making me flinch. Then she took me in her mouth, moving around it like she was obsessed with it. I rolled her over and fucked her mouth with my tongue, working my way down to her mound of pubic hair. She was already wet. I took her clit and massaged it with my tongue. I felt her body start to shudder, ready to cum. Her nails dug into my back, drawing blood, and she gasped and let out a moan. I grasped her hips and rammed myself inside her, pumping back and forth until I exploded.

"She made love to my body with a thousand sins from her lips."

It was like art the way she made love to me. It was dark in the room, but I could see everything except her face. Just her eyes when she looked into mine. They were like fire, making my temperature rise. Then when she came, she whispered my name with a passion I'd never heard from any woman.

We both lay naked on the bed, facing each other, and she played with my face. My hands were running down her hair when I sensed a shadow over us.

"Isn't it just like you, Mother?" Catherine said. "I bring them home, and you fuck them."

I left the house at five in the morning. I wasn't sure why my conscience had kicked in. Then I realized what was bothering me. It wasn't morality at all. Whatever was between Simone and her husband wasn't true love. It wasn't nothing either. Being honest with myself. There was no trick. I think Simone affected me more than I wanted to admit. The woman made my blood boil.

So, now I was on the street in New York, I didn't know a soul, and I just had a briefcase and what I had on. And my American Express card that my mum had given me. That's all I took. I walked the streets of Manhattan for four days with no sleep, just thinking. And it was cold; it was January.

I left Simone's house because I just didn't want to wake up the next morning to eat breakfast with the family, knowing I had just slept with his wife, even though I had no choice. But I decided to leave.

So, I walked Manhattan for days, and then I went into a café and saw a blond woman. I walked up to her and said, "Hello there. I find you very attractive. I want to move in with you; this all I have—my clothes, my briefcase, and myself."

She was shocked. Speechless, she opened her mouth, but no words came out. "But I don't know you," she said.

I said, "I know that, but I have nowhere to go, and you seem like a nice person. And not only that, you intrigue me."

"You're crazy. I don't even know you; you might be a killer or something," she said.

"Look at me. I have nothing to hide and nothing to conceal. This is me. Seize the moment. I have no place to go, and I want to move in with you."

Then we sat and talked. Next thing I knew, I was in her apartment on Eighty-Sixth and Lexington. It was beautiful. I made her the happiest woman alive, and then we started going out and eating in places. The love was beautiful. I thought I was a baby face. I put all my cards in one basket and fell for that woman. She worked; she made the money, but I just stayed home. It was beautiful for a good year.

Then the problems started, the accusations and the mistrust. She would come home, slam doors, get angry, and scream. "Why is my house dirty? Why is this? Why is that? What did you do all day? I'm tired of this."

And this happened day after day and night after night. I knew it was coming. But again, I put all my cards in one basket, which was a wrong move. Then is how the logic of women started to kick in.

Why do women do what they do? What made her do what she did?

It was this simple: she was just tired, and she found someone else who was doing better than I was and who promised her a better lifestyle. I don't care how much a woman loves you; if you are living in her house with no job and no money, it's a matter of time. Even if the sex is great, if you are not bringing anything new, she is either going to kick you out or nag and nag and curse you, and so much that it won't stop. And if she is all you've got, then you're fucked. But again, is she wrong? When there is no money coming from you, she feels like she is carrying all the weight, and you're home doing nothing, even though you're trying. And when it's like this, after a while, she is bound to cheat on you to justify herself, or she'll just leave you alone. For a man, stability and a job is very important in a relationship.

So, she came in one night so angry and started slamming doors. I was laying on the couch.

"Kenneth, we have to talk," she said.

"What is it?" I said.

"I'm tired of this. You have to leave. It's been like this for a year now. You keep saying you will find a job. I keep waiting. I can't do this anymore. You have to leave now."

"But I have nowhere to go," I said.

"Too bad."

So, I packed my suitcase, put on a suit, and left. I held the door, hoping she would call me back or change her mind. Nothing happened.

I got downstairs, back to square one. I put my head on the door and asked myself why I didn't want to call my mother overseas. I said to myself, "But I was faithful; I grew to love her, I honored her, and I adored her. What went wrong?"

As I was thinking, a guy walked up to me and asked whether she was upstairs. I was so numb that I opened my mouth, but the words didn't come. He just looked at me and kept going upstairs.

All the pieces just came together. She was seeing someone else. The situation was that simple: he offered her better, and she accepted.

I came to understand women. Women love powerful men, and they are attracted to a man's wealth and power. That's what's sexy for them, but there is a practical reason behind the attraction.

Men are much more basic and frivolous. Give them tits and ass, and they don't care what's in the bank or in the brains.

I swore to myself I would never let a girl in ever again. I thought I'd never love again. I thought my life was over, and I didn't want to face or even see another day until I decided to be fearless and reinvent myself.

It was like playing Russian roulette, hoping to hit, or having one bullet in a six-shot revolver. You keep clicking and clicking, waiting for that one time that you click, and it kills you.

It's like walking in crowd of people but still feeling alone.

I figured that whenever you're in conflict with someone, there is one factor that can make the difference between damaging your relationship and deepening it. And that factor is attitude. Just don't give up trying to do what you really want to do.

I picked up my phone, and I called Tracy.

She said, "Hello."

I said, "Hi, come pick me up. I'm on Eighty-Sixth between Fourth Avenue and Lexington."

She said okay with no questions asked. I was impressed.

When Tracy got there, she came out her car. She wore this short red dress, with her hair all the way down. She radiated night heat, the sensuous quality in a woman that makes men ache with desire. Her body was made for sin—skin the color of light cinnamon, fiery emerald eyes, and wet red lips. Her legs were long and slender. I think it was her hot Latin blood that made her intensely passionate. She was leaning dangerously over a railing.

I stood behind her and stared at her. I had never made love to a woman like her. Most women either make love to me because of lust or because they want something—clothes, jewels, or the good life. None had ever gotten under my skin until tonight.

This woman was neither impressed with my money nor my looks; this woman was different from any woman I had ever met. It wasn't just that she conveyed an aura of independence but also that she knew she was my equal in every meaning of the word. I sensed it the moment I'd met her at my godmother's house. She was just a pure female, unaffected by what life had to offer.

She leaned against the railing and bent over to pick something up. I watched the sensuous movements of her body, imagining her with no clothes on.

I came up behind her and put my hands on her hips. Her sequined red dress ended several inches above the knee, her long legs were covered by black silk net stockings, and her black cloth shoes had gold-plated spiked heels.

She turned around with vengeance and fury, trying to see who was holding her. She looked at me.

If eyes were windows to the soul, my eyes revealed the good, the bad, the ugly, some dirty deals, and some things I wouldn't want to brag about. Hers were temple doors, hiding secrets.

Our lips met, and I kissed her gently at first, just brushing her lips, and then pressed harder. She pushed me back, her eyes blazing fire. "I don't kiss strange men."

"Neither do I."

"What do you want from me, Ken?" she said.

"You, all of you," I said.

She got in her car, and I got in the passenger seat.

She drove off to her place. When we got there, she got out. I followed her, and as we got into her apartment, I looked around. It was pretty impressive.

She came close to me, ripped my shirt, and kissed me hard.

I pulled her dress up above her hips and lifted her onto my hardness.

As I entered her, I knew I was violating my most sacred principle—never fall in love.

I had spent most of my life avoiding the pain of loss. It was a sickness to love and lose and never want to love again.

But I knew she was the one. I hadn't chosen her; I hadn't thought about what life would be like with her—or without her—or even if she thought the same about me. It had just happened. I knew I couldn't hide behinds my fears anymore and that I wouldn't be able to live without lying in bed at night with her at my side, without seeing her body naked beside mine, without running my hands down her body to the feminine mystery between her legs.

As I held her, as our bodies flowed with the erotic rhythm of lovemaking and her tight body squeezed me inside her, I had a terrible thought, a moment of precognition that made me both sad and frightened.

I would love her, yet I knew I would lose her.

9

Life after that was beautiful. I got in to school and the Interboro Institute. My major was business management. I lived with Tracy, and she was just everything.

I fell hard for her; it was just something about her. There was an essence, a feminine mystique about her that drew me inexorably to her. I felt lost without her.

There was no meaning to life without her. There was no me without her; I just couldn't imagine life without her.

Days without her seemed endless. I found myself sitting there and wanting her. She invoked that feeling in me.

I was waiting for her to give my heart a fresh breath of life because with her, I was stuck in what seemed like a lifeless eternity.

Everything on this lovers' day seemed bitter and bland without the beat of my heart by her side. She became the rhythm in my song, the colors in my sky, the waves in my ocean, and an art that never faded or died.

"Paint me with your colors," I said. "I am your canvas, waiting to become your masterpiece." In short, she was my life.

I was afraid to love, and yet I loved her. My fear was like a wall. I walked right through it. The wall was still there, and yet it didn't stop me. I needed it, and yet I needed her. I needed her without having a reason. But I was still afraid I might lose her or that she might not accept my desperate need.

She was a flower; I was a slender reed.

So, what more could I ask for? I had a good woman, I was in school, and everything was okay.

I got a job at my school as a computer tech; I was an IT guy, going around fixing computers on campus. I was the envy of all my friends. They didn't seem to understand my logic or how I'd gotten Tracy.

When she came to pick me up, my friends went crazy, saying, "You the man." I felt like a superstar. I told them I was the reason. I said that no girl could ever cheat on me. "That is a fact," I said. At least I thought it was.

I just couldn't see a woman cheating on me. I was everything a woman could ask for. To me, cheating on me was technically impossible; it wasn't said. "It just can't happen," I told my friends. "I'm that good," I said.

I mean, even after all this time, she evoked a pain in me that was as sharp as ever. No one had ever touched me as she did. And no one ever would.

It was six o' clock in the morning, and I wiped the sleep from my eyes. It felt just like an ordinary day. But it wasn't. It was my fifteen-month anniversary with her. I watched my lady sleep, and I felt blessed. I was just sitting there, daydreaming about her and all the things she did. It felt so right, and all I knew was that she was the one for me. She stirred and said, "Good morning, babe."

I said, "Morning, boo. Happy anniversary."

She threw her hands around my neck and kissed me. "Happy anniversary, baby. I love you," she said.

I felt like heaven. I said, "Baby, since today is our anniversary, I have a limo picking you up at ten. It's taking you to a spa on Thirty-Fourth Street and Fifth Avenue. Get your hair and nails done; have a body massage. Get a manicure and a pedicure. The whole nine. It's our day, baby."

When she heard that, she jumped on me and kissed me hard. I brought her under me and slowly ran my lips down her body, starting at her neck, caressing her breasts, sucking each nipple in my mouth, and teasing her belly button. Then she spread her legs open and arched her back as I worked my way down to her pubic hair and kissed the swollen lips between her legs. Then my lips traveled back up her body, leaving her laughing and shuddering from delight, until I found her mouth and kissed her again. Then I entered her, giving her everything, but in the mist of our passionate lovemaking, she dug her nails into my back and drew blood.

"I'm about to cum," I said.

She was saying so. She shook, telling me not to stop.

I stopped. I said, "Baby, I'm running late. I have to go to school and then work. Meet me back here in the house at eight. Then we will finish this, and we'll go have dinner."

"Come back, baby. I need you," she said, throwing a pillow at me.

I came back and kissed her, and then I got in the shower, got dressed, and left.

I got to school pretty late and got into class. After my classes, I got ready and picked my friend up, and we went to clock in to start working on campus.

So after that, I was sitting with my best friend, Jay Vargas. We worked together after school to check all the PC computers on campus, and after we were done, we just sat down and talked about women—women in general, the things they did and the lies they told, the conceptions, their envy, and the reasons they did what they did.

A FedEx guy came with mail. I thought it was mail for the school. But the FedEx guy said, "Excuse me, is there a Kenneth Mady here."

"Speaking," I said.

"Can you sign here please."

I was confused. No mail came to my school for me, which made me curious. I took the package from the guy and looked at it. It had my full name but no return address.

I was shocked and confused, but I signed for it anyway.

The FedEx guy left, and my friend said, "What is in it?"

I said, "I have no idea."

He said, "Fuck it. Since we're bored, open it."

So I picked up the box and tore the tape off. My heart skipped a beat. I opened it to see a bunch of wrapping paper, and I dug through it. Then I saw a DVD. I was confused, and my friend looked at me. We had the same look.

He said, "Since we're bored, let's watch it. There is nothing else to do."

"Fuck it; let's watch it," I said.

So, my friend went to go get the TV and the DVD player from the locker room.

I popped the DVD in the DVD player and sat back. My friend sat, took the remote, and pressed play. The first thing that appeared was a guy with a blurry face, and then a woman appeared wearing a red dress. Now, my friend and I were really into the movie or whatever it was.

Then he said, "Malcolm, isn't that your fiancée?"

I looked. It was her. I looked again, and I said to myself, "It can't be." But I was wrong. It was her.

On the DVD, she was taking her clothes off and at the same time, kissing this guy with the blurry face. The guy wasn't me. Then she went down on her knees, unzipped the guy's pants, and took him in her mouth.

I was weak. My eyes were stuck on the TV.

Then the guy shuddered, and he came. She kissed him all over, not missing anything. Then she brought her face to his, and he kissed her again. Then she lay down on the floor, spread her legs apart, and told the guy to climb on top of her. He took his shirt off. Then he entered her and pushed himself back and forth inside her.

She was moaning in a way I had never heard her moan before, calling him names, telling him to fuck her harder, and screaming in a way I never thought she could.

The guy turned her around and fucked her from behind, pulling her hair. It was obvious she was enjoying it from the look in her eyes, the movements of her body, and the use of her tongue.

I never knew I could feel this much pain. It was as if someone had just struck me with a knife. That moment, my soul died. Every emotion in me died in that instant.

Tears ran down my face. I didn't even know I was crying. They were just there.

"I thought you were the great Malcolm," my friend said.

"What happened?"

For the first time in my life, I was speechless. I opened my mouth, but words didn't come out. I took the remote and stopped the tape. I didn't want to watch anymore.

"You okay?" my friend said.

"I'm fine," I said.

"What are you going to do?" he said.

"What can I do? The damage is done."

"You've been played. I told you—play or get played," he said. "You are the fool now. I thought you loved her; I thought she couldn't cheat on you."

I was thinking. My mind wandered. I didn't think Tracy would lie or cheat on me; there had never been anything between us that would cause a need for deception.

But the truth was in front me. She had been making love to another man, doing things I never thought she could do, moaning in a way I never thought she could, exploring the stranger's body in a way that she had never explored mine, and kissing him in places that I never knew could be excited in a man's body.

I felt betrayed; I felt used. Tracy had a hold on me that no one else on earth had.

And the fear of losing her was petrifying to me. But that moment, I had seen her on tape doing things to a stranger. And the mystery of how somebody sent me the tape.

Just watching her on tape killed me, for she was a part of me. Something inside me died.

10

I came home in a cold rage to kill. My friend drove me home since he thought I wasn't in the right state of mind to go home by myself.

"Are you sure you will be fine?" he said.

"Of course," I said, even though I was lying.

"Stay up," he said. "It's okay; it happens to be the best."

"Love." Bores You?"

"No, it disappoints me."

After my friend left, I turned off all the lights and just sat there. I brought out the DVD and put it in my DVD player.

I sat in total darkness, in a quiet rage, for God knows how long. I was just thinking. My head pounded. My eyes were misty. Music played in the background. It was funny; the music that came on was "Maybe I Deserve" by Tank.

I hit all the high points—shock, murderous anger, and mindless jealousy. One moment, I was ready to choke the lies from her, and the next, I had the impulse to cry at her feet and beg her not to leave me.

So many thoughts ran through my mind. I called her acts infidelity, and that's what they were. We weren't married, but we lived together, professed our love for each other, and shared the same bed. I felt a rage unknown to man.

I kept asking myself why. I told myself I had to hear her out, that she had to tell me what was going on.

"Desire is a stranger, you think you know."

I asked myself why she swore eternal love if all she wanted was excitement. I felt like she had just ripped my heart out and thrown it in a vat of acid.

I heard keys in the door, and she walked in. "Hey, baby, I missed you," she said. "Why do you have all the lights off? What's wrong? It's our anniversary. Come on; let's go have a blast."

"Come here, baby; come sit. I have a surprise for you," I said.

She jumped and sat next to me. Giving me a kiss, she said, "I missed you, babe."

So I put my hands around her waist, pulled her close to me, and held her tight.

"What's the surprise, babe? I can't wait," she said.

So I pressed Play on the TV.

"What's this, babe?" she said.

"Your gift. Watch it."

I held on to her tightly; this way, I got to see her facial reactions. The movie came on. Since I had a huge screen TV, the light from it lit the whole place up.

Then she appeared on the TV with her red dress on. She went down on her knees, on all fours, and the guy with the blurry face was smiling while she went down on him.

"What the fuck is this, Ken," she said, her voice shaky.

"You tell me," I said, holding on to her. She pulled away. She struggled and pushed me away, getting up from the couch.

"Tracy, what the hell is going on? How long have you been seeing this guy?"

"What do you care?"

"What the fuck do you mean by *what do I care*? Are you seeing him now?" I said.

"Yes," she said.

"Since when?"

"Since last year. I'm disgusting," she said.

"You are phenomenal; you're so clever. Why are you dating me?"

"I stopped seeing him; I wanted you," she said.

"Why did you tell me you wanted children?" I said.

"Because I did."

"And now do you want children with him?"

"Yes. I don't know."

"But we're happy, aren't we?"

She was stepping back, and I was coming toward her. "Do you think I'm going to hit you? What do you think I am?"

"I have been hit before."

"Not by me," I said.

"So."

"Did you have sex with him?"

"Yes."

"Is he a good fuck?" I said.

"Don't do this," she said.

"Just answer the question. Is he good?" I said.

"Yes."

"Better than me?"

"Different."

"Better."

"Gentler."

"What does that mean?"

"You know what I mean," she said.

"Tell me."

"No."

"I treat you like a whore."

"Sometimes."

"Why would that be?"

"I'm sorry you—"

"Don't say it. Don't you fucking say you're too good for me."

"I am, but don't say it."

I looked into her face. "Wait, did you just have sex with him, take a shower, and come see me? So you wouldn't smell him. So you would feel less guilty. How do you feel?"

"Guilty," she said.

Tears came down my face. "Did you ever love me?"

"Yes," she said. And she came close to me.

I pushed her away from me, walked back into the living room, and looked around.

I turned back to her. "Did you fuck him in my house?"

"No."

"Why not?"

"Do you wish we did?"

"Just tell me the truth."

"Yes, we did it here."

I looked around. "Where?"

"There." She pointed to the couch. I walked over to it.

"On this. We had our first fuck on this. Did you think of me?"

"When?"

She was quiet.

"When did you do it here?"

She was still quiet.

"Answer the fucking question."

"This morning."

I looked at her.

"Did you cum?"

"Why are you doing this?" she said.

"Because I want to know."

"Yes, I came."

"How many times?"

"Twice."

"How?"

"First, he went down on me. And then we fucked."

"Who was where?"

"I was on top. And then he fucked me from behind."

"And that's when you came the second time," I said.

"God," she said. "Why is the sex so important?"

"Because I fucking want to know."

She was going up the stairs to pack a bag, and I was right behind her. She came down toward the door.

"Did you touch yourself while he fucked you?"

"Yes," she screamed. "We do everything that people who have sex do."

"Do you enjoy sucking him off?"

"Yes."

"You like his dick."

"I love it," she said.

"You like him cumming in your face."

"Yes."

"What does it taste like?" I screamed.

"It tastes like you but sweeter," she screamed back.

"That's the spirit; thank you. Thank you for your honesty. Now fuck off, and die, you bitch."

She left. I walked outside and looked up in the sky. Rain started to fall. I wondered whether God was crying for me. Unfortunately, he wasn't.

Unfortunately, finding love is not easy, and holding on to it no matter what kind of relationship you have is hard. Making it last is complicated. Intimacy is a lie we tell ourselves. If you believe in love at first sight, you never stop looking.

11

Truth is a game you play to win.

I got into my car and drove aimlessly. I was beyond mad, so I just drove around thinking, furious.

I got to a strip club in the Bronx called Sin City. When I went in, there were women everywhere of every class—old, young, and middle class—all dancing naked. There were women of different categories and backgrounds. I mean, name them, and they had them all.

I was impressed. One woman caught my eye and kept me tuning in. She looked like a woman who knew how to use her mind, and that's no small accomplishment.

Maybe because my mother had been a strong-willed, intelligent woman, I didn't find myself attracted to women who thought their greatest worth was in bed.

The woman who looked like she knew her own mind caught me staring at her. I signaled to her, and she walked over to me. I told her I wanted her to give me a private dance. She frowned, looked me over, and told me to follow her into a room.

I sat down and watched her dance for me. I never smoked cigarettes, but today, I lit one, smoked it, and at the same time, tipped her while she stripped for me.

"What's this room called?"

"The Paradise Suite."

"How many paradise suites are there?"

"Eight," she said. She finished dancing and started walking out the door.

"Do I have to pay you to talk to me?"

"No, but if you want to tip me, you're welcome to."

I did tip her.

"Thank you," she said.

"I used to come here a million years ago; it was called the Punk Club. The stage was…"

"Everything is a virgin of something else fifteen years ago."

"How old were you?"

"Four."

"Christ, when I was in flares, you were in nappies."

"My nappies were flared."

"You have the face of an angel."

"Thank you."

"What does your cum taste like?"

"Heaven."

"How long you have been doing this?"

"Three months."

"Nice wig."

"Thank you."

"Does all this turn you on?"

"Sometimes."

"Liar."

"Are you telling me it turns you on because you think that's what I want to hear? Do you think I'm turned on by it turning you on?"

"Doesn't the thought of me creaming myself when I strip for strangers turn you on?"

"Hey, hey, what can I say?"

She bent over, revealing her nakedness to me.

"Are you flirting with me?"

"Maybe."

"Are you allowed to flirt with me?"

"Sure."

"Really?"

"No, I'm not. I'm breaking all the rules."

"You're playing with me."

"Yes, I'm allowed to flirt."

"To price my money from me."

"To price your money from you, I may do or say as I please."

"Except touch."

"You are not allowed to touch."

"Open your legs. Wider."

She did a split, showing me her most sacred place. I came closer.

"Show me."

She pulled her panties apart. This way, I could see better.

"So, what would happen if I touched you now?"

"I would call security."

"And what would they do?"

"They would ask you to leave and not come back."

"And if I refused to leave?"

"They would remove you."

"I will try my best not to touch you. I would like to touch you later."

"I'm not a whore."

"I wouldn't pay."

"Why are you calling yourself Diamond?"

"Because it's my name."

"We both know it isn't."

"You all are protecting your identities."

"There is a girl out there who calls herself Venus."

"What's her real name?"

"Pluto," she said.

"You are cheeky."

"Would you like me to stop being cheeky?"

"No."

"Have you ever desired a customer?"

"Yes."

"Well, put me out of my misery. Do you desire me? Because I'm pretty fucking lost about my feelings for you."

"Your feelings."

"Whatever."

"No, I don't desire you."

"Thank you. Thank you sincerely for your honesty."

"If I ask you to strip right now."

"Would you?"

"Of course. You want me to."

"No."

"Tell me something true."

"Lying is the most fun a girl could have without taking her clothes off. But it's better if you do."

"You are cold, real cold, at heart."

"Where are you from?"

"Las Vegas."

"Why did you leave?"

"Problems with a male."

"Boyfriend?"

"Kind of."

"When you left him. Just like that."

"It's the only way to leave. 'I don't love you anymore, good-bye.'"

"Supposedly, you do still love them."

"You don't leave."

"You've never left someone you still love."

"No."

"Do you have a boyfriend now?"

"Yes."

"How long were you dating him?"

"I wasn't dating him; I was fucking him."

"So, how long were you having sex with him?"

"About a year and a half."

"So why aren't you with him now? Why are you here naked in front of me instead of being with him?"

"Story of my life—I was with him last night, we went to a bar, we had a drink together, he left, and I came here."

"So who was with you last night?"

"No one."

"I wasn't in the mood last night."

"How would you describe your relationship with your boyfriend?"

"I had sex with him for a year and a half; I liked having sex with him. He wasn't afraid of experimenting, and I like men like that. Men who give me pleasure. He gave me a lot of pleasure."

"You like playing games, don't you?"

"Not really."

"Tell me something about yourself that nobody knows."

"I don't wear any underwear. And I don't confess all my secrets just 'cause a guy makes me have an orgasm."

"Really."

"Yes, really."

"Take me home, Ken."

12

"Love is an accident waiting to happen."

I wanted to get away for a weekend and clear my head. I had so much on my mind, so I drove to Atlantic City. As I came up the steps of a casino, I headed for a roulette table on the other side of the casino. I loved the excitement of casinos, all that lush money and the naked desire for it. But I didn't like to gamble. A universal law of mathematics turned me off from tossing my own money on the green felt table; the odds always favored the house. For everyone who had a run of luck and won a few bucks, a hundred others lost.

I sat down at a roulette table, tossed a wad of bills across for chips, and ordered vodka. Despite my aversion to gambling, casinos were a great place to do business and clear your head. My buy-in at the roulette table wasn't looking so good. Then I felt someone sit next to me.

I grinned at Andeshia. "We meet again."

"Life's full of coincidences."

"Maybe it's fate that our trails keep crossing. Aren't there people in India who think everything's predestined, that people's kismet determines what their destinies will be?"

I leaned closer to her, drinking in the arousing scent of her perfume. “Do you suppose that you and I are meant to be lovers?”

She leaned closer to me, until her lips were only a kiss away. “If that’s true,” she whispered, “I will cut my wrists.” She got up and walked away, and I followed her across the casino floor.

I said to her, “Is there is something about me that caused you to hate me on sight? Or are you a bitch to everyone?”

She stopped and faced me. “I’d like to get some air. Would you take a walk with me?”

I hid my surprise behind a blank look and followed her out of the inner sanctum. Crossing the gaming floor, she asked, “I notice you don’t have much interest in gambling.”

“It’s rigged for the house. I’d rather try my luck at something with an even playing field.”

It wasn’t easy, not when dealing with a woman who was much more intelligent than I was. I admired people like Andeshia who had that refined, finishing school, political and social-awareness upbringing.

We went out of the casino and walked along the wooden boardwalk that ran along the ocean. I would just as soon have stayed inside where there were lights and action, but my chances of making it with this beautiful woman were better under a romantic moon than casino lights.

She stopped and touched my face, her cool fingers caressing my cheeks.

I kissed her hand and held it against my chest. I pulled her to me and kissed her. My lips melted into hers. I felt the kiss down to my groin. After the kiss, she stared at me intently for a moment and then let me kiss her again. With her breasts pressed against me, my blood surged.

She drew away from me and walked slowly down the boardwalk. She paused and leaned against the railing. A cool breeze teased us and made the night magical.

"Malcolm—"

"Call me Kenneth. If we are going to be lovers, it will look funny if we don't use first names."

We were entering the casino when something occurred to me. "You said there is a reason you don't trust me. What's the reason?"

"You are too damn attractive. There is something about a good-looking bastard that attracts a woman." She frowned at me. "Even one that should know better." She offered me her hand to shake. "I have got to get back to work."

I took her hand and pulled her to me. "I'm not shaking hands and driving off. This isn't New York; you can't step out of a restaurant and into a taxi. I like you; do you like me?"

She looked deeply into my eyes. "I don't know. What are your intentions, Ken?"

"To show you something different, a different lifestyle."

We lay in the bed the next morning, and Andeshia's body pressed snugly against mine. I felt warm and comfortable.

I don't have a rating system for all the woman I have fucked, but making love to Andeshia had been different than the others. It wasn't that my blood boiled hotter or even the numbers of times I got it up, and we got it off. It was something else. As I lay in that warm cozy twilight between sleep and being awake, I tried to understand what it was exactly.

Then it came to me—peace. I felt at peace, as if being with Andeshia satisfied some deeper urge than I had felt with any other woman.

"Babe, let's go to Paris."

"Are you serious?"

"Yes, let's just get away and get to know each other. You'll get to shop, dance, eat in a French restaurant, and make love on a warm beach."

"Okay, you have convinced me."

"No, I think you need more convincing. Come under the covers; I have something for you."

Andeshia said, "I will go buy the tickets. Call your mum for a discount; doesn't she work for an airline?"

"Yes, I will call her."

We took a flight to Paris from Newark, New Jersey, and got there in sixteen hours through British Airways.

We checked into a suite at the Hotel du Louvre. Andeshia marveled at the elegance and quaintness of the luxury hotel.

This stylish and elegant boutique hotel stands at the heart of Paris culture and arts. Each one of the Hotel du Louvre's four facades looks out at a famous Parisian landmark—the Louvre Museum, the Opera Garnier, the Comédie Française, and the Place du Palais Royal. This area is rich in history, and the hotel's second-empire architecture is mirrored by the surrounding buildings in this special quarter of Paris.

I pulled Andeshia to me. "Let's have dinner in bed."

"No, no, this is my chance to eat in a real restaurant."

We ate at the best French restaurant in Paris. We ended up having dessert in bed.

The next morning, we took a taxi downtown to a gem dealer. I left Andeshia in the cab and told her I would be back in a few minutes. When I came back out, I shoved a thick wad of bills into her purse.

"What's that for?"

"Exotic see-through lingerie, captivating perfume…hell, get a tiger-skin coat or something."

She gave the money back to me.

"I'm not taking the money back. Put it in a poor box or something if it bothers you so much. I will meet you in the hotel in a couple of hours."

"It's too much money."

"Don't worry. It's not my money; I stole it."

Just joking.

13

Passion is not so much an emotion as a destiny. For desire, even in its wildest tantrums, can neither persuade me. For the heart wants what it wants.

I was in a good mood when I got back to the hotel. We had dinner in our room that evening.

"Why are you so frightened to get involved with a man?"

"Is that what we are—involved?"

She reached over and placed her hands on my neck, slipping her fingers down inside my open collar and gently caressing the flesh. It was so gentle and so unlike her regular touch that it brought up chills all over my back, and it stirred passion I never knew existed in me.

I lay in bed that night with her head on my shoulder and her soft warm breathing against my neck. Neither of us were in any mood for wild, passionate sex. We just cuddled close.

I tried to analyze my feelings for Andeshia. Were they lust? Love? Passion? Sympathy? Now that I had gotten what I wanted—the velvet rubbed off my dick, as my friend would say—was I ready to move on?

No great revelation came. But one thing puzzled me. I wanted to be with her, not just for the moment. I wanted to make her proud of me and to protect her. But I had never felt this way before.

14

We took a flight back to New York two days later. She started asking me personal questions, and I kissed her hand. "I don't ask questions about your past." I kissed her cheek and brushed her lips with mine. We were approaching New York.

"Now tell me the truth. The moment you get off this airplane, you are going to forget you even know me."

"Never." I kissed her nose. "I have never felt about anyone like I do about you." That was the truth.

We left the plane and walked together into the terminal. A surprise was waiting for me. A woman was holding up a handkerchief with the name *Ken* chalked on it in lipstick. It was Simone.

"Oh shit." I thought I'd muttered it under my breath, but it came out. "I can explain," I told Andeshia.

The look on her face told me there was no way I could explain.

"Hello, forgive me for my little joke." Simone shook hands with me and Andeshia. She said to me, "I'm sorry I showed up unexpectedly. I tried to reach you. But I was told you were out the country."

"I will be with you in a moment."

I escorted Andeshia to a taxi. I gestured at one at the cabs and paid the driver to take her home.

"You have slept with her, haven't you?"

It wasn't a question. There was nothing I could say.

She left angry and hurt. As I watched the taxi leave, Simone appeared beside me.

"Did I say something wrong?"

"You are a bitch."

She kissed me on the mouth. "Of course I am. But at least I'm good at it. It's the only way a woman can deal with men who think they are in charge of the world."

"What are you here for? Did you drop in on your broom to ruin my life?"

She laughed. "Oh no, please, don't tell me that the dashing and glamorous Ken has fallen in love—and with an idealistic little bookworm. At least you could leave me for a movie star."

"I can't leave someone I never had."

We got into a taxi together.

"Is it going to complicate matters if I stay at the same hotel that you and Andeshia are in?" she asked.

"Andeshia is meeting friends from work, and I'm busy doing business this afternoon."

"Good. I was worried I was going to spoil your evening."

"You are not. I'm taking you to your hotel and dropping you off. I have a hectic afternoon to consider."

She put her hand on my upper thigh. "You are angry at me. I really am sorry."

She squeezed the top of my leg. I disliked this woman, but her touch sent my blood pressure up. What fools men are.

Her hand went back to my thigh and squeezed; she leaned against me and kissed me. Her lips were warm and lush.

"What can I do to make all this up to you?" she asked.

I laughed. She got out the taxi and slammed the door. She started to walk away and turned back, speaking to me through the open window.

She hesitated. "Don't hate me."

Simone got to her hotel, undressed, and took a bath, and then she showered afterward and applied bath oil to her damp body. Sitting naked in front of the mirror, she finished putting on her makeup. She lubricated her vagina with a sperm killer, then put on lacy white panties and a bra. The color contrasted well with her copper-toned complexion.

Before she put on her dress, she posed in front of a full-length mirror and let out a sigh. Men would describe her as sexy and sensuous, but like most women, Simone was her own worst critic.

She chose a red strapless cotton dress, nice enough for evening but not as provocative as she would have worn for a cocktail party.

When she was done, she left the room and took the elevator up two floors to the ground floor; I don't know how she knew I was there. I was discussing business with a few guys when she walked up behind me and tapped my shoulder.

I turned around swinging to see who it was because I hate people tapping me, but she weaved it, came under my hands, and kissed me. I was shocked and breathless at the same time.

I leaned down and kissed her and ran my lips down her neck and breathed in the floral essence between her breasts. "Hmm, you smell like a woman should."

She returned the kiss with eagerness. "Are you still mad at me?"

I was speechless. I came to realize that it's crazy to love someone who hurts you. But it's crazier to think that someone who hurts you loves you.

I decided to go someplace new and start all over. So, I bought a ticket for a three-week stay in Vegas. I wanted to try my luck and see what God had to offer me in Vegas.

I left on a Friday morning.

Before I boarded the plane, I had three missed calls from Andeshia. She left a message. But I wasn't in the mood to listen to it. So, I left for Las Vegas.

15

I went to Las Vegas for the first time, and I thought God lived there. Everything was different—the people, the cars, even the women in Vegas had dresses that molded to their bodies and exposed the luscious curves of their breasts. They smelled like expensive sex, Chanel No. 5. Even the men had an expensive smell. And Vegas had the song of money; I had never heard the song before, not this loud at least. But on the strip, the music was numbing and seductive, putting you into a dream state. It filled your ears all the way down the boulevard—the rattle of dice and cries at the craps, the sounds of cards being shuffled at the blackjack tables, the clatter of a roulette ball bouncing around the wheel, and the hum of thousands of slot reels spinning, silver flushing from them.

Something spiritual entered my body and glowed inside me that night.

I looked up into the sky, and for the first time in my life, I told God, "I'm going to make it. Someday. Sometime. Somewhere."

I came to realize that people didn't dream there. But Vegas was different. It was like a Hollywood set, a place where dreams came true. Not for everyone, but once in a while, someone threw down a bet or pulled a slot handle and won a big jackpot.

That night in Las Vegas was amazing, I loved Vegas; it was like Hollywood. What I liked about Vegas was the vibration—you felt it everywhere you went, driving down the strip or Fremont Street, walking through the casinos, sitting in the restaurants, hell, even getting gas at a self-service convenience store. The vibration came from the sound of money. There was no other place in the world where money made a louder noise than in Vegas.

A few guys took me to a bar where there were a few strippers dancing at the bar. After all, it was Vegas. We took a table and ordered drinks. There were several lap dancers doing their thing when a few women came over to us to see who the big spender was.

"May I dance for you?" she asked one of the guys.

Lap dancing was personal. The guy who paid for the dance got the heat.

A girl entered the room, and my eye caught hers, and she came to the table. She had light skin, long hair, and an adorable face; there was a mystery to her face and green eyes.

She smiled. "I'm Erika. May I dance for you?"

"Please," I said a little too eagerly.

When she started moving her body to the beat of the music, everything faded around me in the bar except for her. I felt as if someone had turned off the lights and shut down the noise, leaving only a bright spotlight on her. But this girl moved fluidly, seductively, like a queen cobra slithering to the subtle tone of a flute. She stripped down to her scarlet brassiere and panties. Her nipples were ready to jut out of the thin silk bra. She removed the brassiere slowly to reveal a cornucopia of succulent flesh, firm but lush, not too big but more than a mouthful. Her green eyes teased me as she got closer and closer. I felt the heat surging in my body. Then she stepped out of her sheer silk panties to reveal the soft, fleshy mound that had been shaved. There was something wetly erotic about a shaved pubis.

I've always wondered why statues of men and women never show pubic hair. I figure it's because bodies are so much more sensual when that part is naked.

I looked into those laughing green eyes and wanted to taste those red lips so badly—both sets—I was ready to do the unspeakable. This girl, Erika, didn't just get my blood pumping; she got under my skin and into my head.

She took it all off until she was naked down to her red nail polish.

And when she finished dancing, I pulled fifty bucks out of my pocket and handed it to her.

She looked at me. "Another dance."

I figured I had no more money on me. So I said, "No thanks."

She said, "Enjoy your drink."

Her voice sent shivers up my spine. I got up and was walking out of the bar. I turned to look at Erika. Contempt, that's what she had for me; contempt because I didn't have the price of a dance. I smiled to myself. "Women."

A couple of weeks after being put down by Erika, I saw her walking into one of the casinos. I followed her and found her inside, methodically losing money at a quarter machine.

"Hey there; long time no see."

She glanced at me. It wasn't not a real look, just a sideways glance. She wore a tank top that displayed her nipples.

"I'm not interested; get a life."

I grinned. "You are making a mistake. You don't know who you're talking to. I'm the great Ken, the one and only. If you are really nice to me, I will buy you a fur coat to warm up that cold personality of yours."

She looked at me and said, "What would you buy it with, your nails? Go fuck yourself, Ken."

I put my hand in my pocket, brought out a quarter, flipped it, and caught it. Then I put it in the slot machine and pulled the handle.

I then turned to her and said, "It's sad that you are pathetic, but I like your spirit."

When I looked back at the machine. The tumblers stopped on a jackpot emblem, then a second one, and a then third. A light flashed above the machine, and a fog horn went off. I stared stupidly at the three medallions on the pay line and the list of winning combinations. I had just won my first jackpot ever—three thousand dollars from a quarter slug.

Erika leaned over, and her hot wet tongue licked my ear. "Can I take you home?"

I smiled. Story of my life.

We went to her place. Erika's place was the usual one-bedroom Vegas apartment. She poured into my arms the moment we stepped into her apartment. I kicked the door shut as I was kissing her. Her body was hot and solid, firmer than any woman I'd been with. She yanked her tank top over her head and pushed her skin-tight blue jeans down, leaving her standing in a silky white bra and panties. We moved our way to the couch in between our kissing and my stripping.

I undid her bra and buried my face against her lush melons. Chanel No. 5 robbed me of my senses. Her nipples were distended with excitement. I took one in my mouth while my hands pulled off the white panties, and I moaned with delight. I had never felt a naked pussy like hers.

"Eat me," she cried.

My lips found her clit, and I worked into a frenzy of passion, and she grabbed the back of my head and pulled me in deeper and deeper as she spread her legs, grinding her hips and arching her back. As soon as she exploded, she was ready again, pushing me back onto the couch and mounting me. I stood up, holding her buttocks in both hands, letting her ride my erection, and pulling her back so my cock rubbed against her clit. She grabbed me by the side of my head and bit my mouth as she came again.

Erika knew she was high-class sex. Don't get me wrong—she had street sex-appeal, the stark sexuality of a cocktail waitress exposing some tits and ass as she bends over to serve your drink. But at the same time, Erika was a class act, a woman wrapped in pearls and sable getting out of a Rolls Royce. My first impression of her was of a cheetah with a diamond choker, a long slender white cat with black spots that hunts alone.

My friend asked what I thought about her.

I said, "I wouldn't kick her out of bed."

Erika woke me up, and she said we were going out. I got dressed, and I followed her out the door, toward her car.

"I like your car. Makes you established," I said.

She said, "Yes, it's a Bentley."

"That must have cost you almost a mil."

She rolled her eyes; it was a dumb question. A woman like her didn't pay for anything. She took one look at the car I had rented from the airport and stopped. "We're taking my car."

"Embarrassed to be seen in mine?"

"Yes."

She threw me the keys of the Bentley, and I climbed in. I got it out the driveway without denting the fenders and drove in silence for a minute, but I wasn't someone who let dead dogs lie, or whatever the expression is. "Listen, I'm not a car person."

"You also don't know anything about clothes."

"Look, lady—"

"No, you look. Vegas is as phony as Hollywood. If you want to be big time in this town, you have to act the part. We are stopping at the Gucci store."

"What's wrong with the way I'm dressed?" I was wearing my best suit. It was a medium-quality ready-made suit.

"Tonight we are mingling with the rich and famous. Do you want to look like one of them or an employee?"

I was ready to tell her to take her sweet ass out and go fuck herself. Then she leaned over and put her hand on my thigh. My blood started pounding.

"Ken, I know what you want—respect, money, to be somebody. But you will never get those things just by working hard. In this town, you only get them if you look like you have money. Money breeds money. If you want me around, you are going to have to look like you are somebody."

Women? It's simple when you have money; women come to you, for whatever reason.

Erika and I had fun that day; we went shopping and gambling and had a blast. I took her home and went back to my hotel. Weeks passed, and I didn't hear from her or see her. I called and got no answer.

I had three days left in Vegas before I flew back to New York. For some reason, Erika had disappeared. I didn't see her, and I was devastated. I felt like she'd used me. And I really fell for her; I liked her.

The day I was to fly back to New York, I called her. A guy picked up and said she was at her wedding reception.

I was shocked. She'd never said she was engaged or about to get married. I really felt used, which is unlike me.

I called her phone. The same guy picked up, and I asked him for the address of the wedding reception. He told me.

I drove over there. My flight was leaving in three hours. I got to her wedding reception, and I signaled a woman and told her to tell the bride, "Ken is in the next room and needs to see you urgently."

Brides always look radiant on their wedding days, but Erika was a knockout in her wedding dress. She was truly beautiful. Her warm sex appeal radiated.

She came in without knocking and slammed the door behind her. "How dare you interrupt my wedding with a command?"

"How dare you play with my emotions and my feelings? This is not *Days of Our Lives*."

This is my feelings? This is real life? That's like putting a candy in front of a child? And taking the candy away? The child will cry?

"You used me, Erika."

"It's Vegas, Ken," she said. "I wanted you, but you live a thousand miles away in New York, and I'm here. We live two different lifestyles. I have to go, Ken; I'm getting married."

"It's America. What can I say?" I pulled her toward me, and she immediately began to squirm out of my arms, ready to slap my face, but I caught her hand just in time. "Why are you fighting me? I know you want me." She bit my hand. "You want to play rough, I can play rough too." I pushed her up against the wall, and then I kissed her. I shoved my tongue against her teeth. She opened them long enough to clench down and bite, and I pulled her dress up and was surprised to find she had nothing on underneath her dress. Her nakedness excited me even more.

She said, "Ken, take me."

She bit my tongue again so hard that I tasted blood.

I kissed her again, and then my hand found her clit. She was soaking wet; she let out a moan. I put my finger inside her, and her fluids came and made her slippery wet with excitement. She let out a loud moan, and her body shuddered against me.

Her tongue now shoved past my lips, and her arms came around my neck as I unzipped my pants and brought myself out. I was ready to cum any minute, so I entered her. She let out a gasp. My hands were on her firm butt as I lifted her up and down my hard shaft.

I exploded into her, and our bodies pressed together. Both of us were breathless in the throws of ecstasy. I looked at her face, still holding her close to me. Her eyes were closed.

I slowly brought her down. She looked at me, kissed me and walked out to go get married.

16

Attraction isn't a choice. Either you are attracted to someone or you're not.

I flew back to New York. As I was leaving JFK's terminal, Andeshia was standing there, holding a cardboard sign with my name written in lipstick. She thought it was funny. I walked up to her and kissed her.

She said, "Ken, why am I here?"

"Why can't I get you out my mind?"

She drove me to her house. When we got in, I came close to her.

"You haven't changed, Ken."

She was about to swing at me. Then she started punching my chest and screaming, "Why do I love you so much?" But I grabbed her wrist and pulled her to me. This time, she hardly put up a struggle. She smelled good. Her red lips were moist and inviting. Someone once told me that a man's attracted to a woman's lips because her sex organs are entered through the pink lips between her legs. Whatever the reason, I have always been a lip man. And Andeshia had lips I wanted to kiss—in both places. I wanted to make love to her at this time, and I wanted her to love me back. She radiated something more sensuous and exotic.

Andeshia tried to push me away, but not with any real effort. The moment I got close to her, a ripple of heat ran through her, and her nipples swelled with desire. Damn him! It had been that way since the first time she saw me on the airplane. She had loved me from the first moment she saw me. But I had always been insensitive to her feelings, and she tried to hate me for it, but she couldn't keep up the pretense.

I was a maniac, and my intense passion lit fires in her. I had her clothes off, scattered down the hallway and on the bedroom floor, by the time I laid her on the bed. I knelt beside the bed and pushed her legs apart. I started with my tongue on her belly, caressing around her belly button with its hot tip and moving up her bare skin to her chest. My hot tongue teased her swollen nipples, dipped between her breasts, and moved up to her neck. She quivered as my warm lips nibbled her neck. Then I moved back down, slowly touching and tasting every part of her body down to the soles of her feet, before moving back up to where her hot moist womanhood waited for me.

She wanted me, wanted my tongue inside her, wanted my maleness to fill her and join with her in the rhythm of love, but my lips caressed the insides of her thighs instead, working their way slowly closer, inch by inch, to the swollen lips between her legs.

Finally, she couldn't stand it. Her legs widened involuntarily, and her back arched as she reached down and pulled my head deep between her legs.

"Come inside me," she whispered.

The next day, I wanted to surprise Andeshia, so I went to her job, and I had a dozen white roses with one red rose in the middle. She was delightfully surprised to see me waiting for her with a dozen white roses.

She looked exquisite. She wore a silky dark-red dress that came down to her ankles. A seductive slit went up to her thighs. Her hat was small and round, with a mesh veil that fell over her face. A single string of priceless pink Indian pearls showed between the high collars of the dress. She looked like a model in an issue of *Vogue.* Her perfume attacked my senses. One look at her, and I forgot why I had come.

"I wore this dress especially for you."

I raised my eyebrows. "Then take it off."

"No, the color. Red is the color of luck."

"Then what's white?"

"White is the color of death and mourning."

Hmm, I didn't know what she meant. "You smell sweet," I said. "You smell like Eve in the garden."

"Romance by Gucci."

"Marilyn Monroe had the best way of wearing perfume."

"Which was?"

"She said it was the only thing she wore to bed."

I leaned close and brushed her lips with mine. "I thought so. Cool and sweet. You are an oasis."

I wanted to bring romance to this woman. So I took her to the seaport in Manhattan, rented a boat, and led her down to the interior of the boat, which was surprisingly cozy and warm. It was still light out, but the heavy curtains were drawn, and white candles that gave off a pleasant rose scent were burning. On the floor was a flowered quilted mattress with several dozen small pillows.

Standing in the center of the snug room, I felt the warmth of her body and smelled her scent next to mine, and the heat began to run through my body. I stared into her eyes for a moment and then lifted her head and kissed her on the mouth, softly at first, then with ardent passion. We moved over to the mattress, and our clothes came off quickly; neither one of us was ashamed of our nakedness.

"I want to give you a massage. Lie on your stomach," she said.

She spread warm oil on my back and began kneading my flesh with her hands, then massaging my buttocks and legs. The smooth kneading almost put me to sleep. She made me turn on my back and started again with my feet and worked up, gently massaging my testicles. I felt myself growing hard after her silken hand started stroking me. A voracious hunger consumed me, and I lowered her onto my hardened phallus. She moved rhythmically back and forth, up and down, keeping in motion with the rocking swells of the boat. Then she began to move feverishly as the climatic shudders shook her body. The explosion came from my body a moment later. We pressed our bodies together and closed our eyes and let the swaying of the boat rock us to sleep.

We woke up, put on robes, and went to sit on the boat to watch the ocean. Each of us had different thoughts going through our mind.

She turned and looked at me. She said, "Ken, when you left me in New York, I was mad at you. I met someone else, but I left him 'cause of you."

"I'm listening," I said.

"I was in his house, and I took a shower. I had taken special care with my bathing because I wanted to make the night a special one for Travis. He had everything going for him but my love. I have been faking my orgasms since the day I met him. And I'm not a good actress. He worked long and hard at the lovemaking, holding his own reward back to give me pleasure.

"I know that you are a bastard, Ken. Travis was better looking and better mannered. But I was still faking my orgasms.

"It was your fault, Ken. I've loved you since the first time I saw you on that airplane. You're a cocky, rude, pushy guy who walks around like he owns the world. No sane woman would love you, but I do love you. Even after you humiliated me.

"I have twice chosen men who were kinder, gentler, more sophisticated, and better educated. And I had to fake my orgasms because the only man who ever made me cream my pants was you, Ken."

We sat there holding each other while we watched the sun rise, both in our own thoughts.

17

How do you learn to hate someone who richly deserves it?

Unconditional love is just psychobabble. Anyone who gives unconditional love without getting the same in return needs his or her head examined.

Is this simple: people don't change unless they want to. You either have to accept a person or find someone else with the qualities you want.

The hardest thing is feeling so much for a woman who doesn't return your feelings.

Love is a strange phenomenon. I came to understand that you don't choose who you love. Choosing implies rational behavior, and there is nothing rational about love.

Logic and reasoning have nothing to do with love.

Ask any one of the thousands of women whose husbands have used them as punching bags or the men whose wives have taken the gold mine, and they got the shaft.

The only conclusion to reach about a man who abuses his women is that there is something wrong with the woman for her to stay with him and not leave him. For a woman would never leave you if she knew she was the center of your world, even if you caused her unbearable pain.

For she will say, "Even the deepest pain can heal." Which is true, but she will never be the same again. But it will come to a time that she will become fed up.

And once she is fed up, she will leave. And I mean leave for good.

Knowing a woman is one thing, but being with her is another thing. Being married to her is a different ball game.

I came to realize that you can never know a woman fully, and neither can a woman know a man fully. It's just a hidden secret of life that people refuse to reckon with.

I remember meeting a woman, and I said, "I love you."

She looked at me and said, "You don't even know me. How could you love me? You're so full of shit," she said.

I said, "I don't have to know you to love you. Eventually, I will know you, or you will tell me what you want me to know about you. And that's just a fact of life. You will never tell me everything about you, so if I say that I like you, then I like you. If I say that I love you, then I love you. It's that simple. And I don't have to know you to like or love you. 'Cause the fact is that you could be married to a woman for ten years and still have no idea who she is. You might think you do. But you only know what she wants you to know. That's why after ten years, you will be wondering what happened. You'll think, 'I thought I knew her. How could she do this to me? I was married to her for ten years; what happened?'"

That's the hidden secret of life; you can't never know a woman fully unless she wants you to.

It applies both ways. A woman can never know a man fully. Even if she's married to him for twenty years. After so long, she would swear she knows him. But she is wrong. Because when he cheats or kills or does unspeakable things, she'll say, "What happened? How could he do this to me? I thought I knew him." So, she becomes confused and wonders what went wrong.

It's just life. Everyone has a story. Everybody has one, rich, poor, or old.

And every woman has a secret she takes to the grave without telling a soul. Something about her past that she'd rather take to the grave than tell anyone. It could be anything.

Same thing for a man. Every man has a story, something about his past or present that he'd rather keep to himself, and he will take it to his grave.

Growing up, I came to understand that your past always hunts you, even if you've changed.

For example, if I meet an awesome woman, and everything goes so well (I mean, she is just perfect) that I'm ready to marry her. But someone in her past knows her. And she use to be a prostitute. And he tells me.

Nine times out of ten, it might damage my feelings for her. It also depends on how I feel about her. I might disregard it, or I might leave her.

Applies to men too. I once knew a man who met this woman. He loved her. She loved him so much. I mean, her love could move mountains. But three years into the relationship, she was cleaning the house. And she found papers about him going to jail for manslaughter in the first degree for killing his wife. She was devastated. She put the papers on the bed and left him without a word or a call or anything.

That was his past. He came to me and cried. He said, "Ken, what do I do? She left me." Then he told me the story.

He said, "Ken, what should I have done?"

How can you tell the woman you love or you want to be with that you were in jail for killing your wife? Of course she won't be with you.

That's a fact.

But women tell me they have to decide whether they would be with the guy or not. It's not for the guy to make that decision.

That's true.

But it's America.

I know if you tell any woman that, nine times out of ten, she won't be with you.

But on the other hand, if a man finds out that his wife or girl was in jail for killing her husband or boyfriend, he might not be that reluctant to leave her. If he really cares about her.

He might be scared if he didn't know about it. But if she tells him some story or that it was her past and she's changed, his chances of staying with her are high.

Back to my book about why women do what they do.

Women do what they do because men allowed them to do it. And this is what makes them very good at it.

Hmm, Andeshia was in my life and wanted to stay for good. But I came to realize that every woman I had ever been with or come across, for some odd reason, wanted to be in my life. They never wanted to leave.

I didn't really know you could actually fall in love with two women. But was it love or lust or just infatuation?

Story of my life.

18

Claudia Bailey walked in to my life as if she owned me. She showed me that she was equal to me in every meaning of the word. She was 100 percent Jamaican, with an exquisite look about her and eyes that could melt souls. I fell for her the instant we met. She had been a budget manager for a company called BAM in Brooklyn for twelve years. She was a very distinguished lady.

She looked at me and said, "Ken, I'm spoken for. I live in Canarsie. I'm a very independent woman."

"How long have you been with whoever you're with?" I said.

"Five years of heaven and hell. Do you want me?"

Her bluntness intrigued me. Her confidence and aggressiveness arouse me; she was unlike any other woman—there was something different about her. She had a dangerous edge to her personality—a certain aura of strength and power. I found myself intrigued and certainly aroused by her, even though she was fifteen years older than me.

Claudia appeared to be exceptional, and she interested me in a new kind of way.

The first day I met her, I knew I had to undress her. I mean, I had dreams about making love to her, with the thought of her naked body under me.

My dreams were vivid. This woman affected me in every sense of the word. She made my blood pound and my temperature rise.

I lay on my bed one evening; no one was around, but she was in my head. This was very unusual, at least for me. I closed my eyes and imagined making love to this woman.

She appeared in front of me and faced me. I said her name once, very quietly. Then without further ado, I peeled the sensuous sheath of a black silk shirt from her body with expert, strong hands.

She felt like a swimmer about to take the plunge—expectant, excited, and ready to excel.

My hands were big, and my fingers were long and firm. Slowly, I explored her body, brushing her skin until I hooked into her bikini panties—the only other garment she wore—and drew them past her thighs, her calves, and her ankles.

She was naked, but I remained dressed, merely loosening my clothes.

With great care, I pushed her down onto the couch, took my brandy glass, dipped my index finger into the shimmering liquid, and brought it first to the nipple of her left breast, and then to the right one.

The liquor stung, but only for a second. With hardly a pause, I started to suck it from her, making her sigh with pleasure. She threw her arms behind her head and stretched luxuriously. I cupped her breasts together and flicked my tongue across both nipples.

"Take your clothes off," she murmured urgently.

I laughed. "Such impatience."

Keeping both hands on her breasts, I traced my tongue down her body. She writhed with excitement and called out my name.

I opened her thighs by pushing my head between them.

"I want to feel your body."

She murmured, "Please..."

My tongue, like my fingers, was thick, slow moving, and experienced.

"Oh...yes..." She moaned.

Her legs parted even more as she felt the tenseness of the past, prepared for release, and got ready to explode.

I paused to flavor my tongue with brandy while my hands continued to work on her breasts.

She felt the sting of the alcohol, the expertise of my fingers, and the strength of my tongue.

"Oh God, Ken. This is so great. This is heaven—oh..." She hit her climax hard. And it was worth waiting for. I buried my head between her legs and enjoyed every hot throbbing moment.

She told me she had seen the good, the bad, and the ugly of lovemaking. But when it came to me, I showed her a different world, a different art of lovemaking. She said that I am an interesting lover. I smiled. Story of my life.

I opened my eyes, looked around, and whispered her name—"Claudia." But she wasn't there. My fingers were cold. But I was sweating.

I told myself, "I can't love two exceptional women." Andeshia was still in my life. Claudia was entering my life with a force unknown to man.

Then it hit me, with all my experience.

"You can never understand love."

My friend said, "What makes Claudia so different, so exceptional?"

I said, "She is interesting. 'Cause I appreciate and admire a fine body regardless of the make. And the main thing is her eyes. She has those eyes that can look right through the bullshit to the good in someone."

"Thirty percent angel."

"Seventy percent devil. And she is down to earth and isn't afraid to get a little engine grease under her fingernails. But Claudia has so much going for her, so it is skeptical."

She looked at me and said, "Ken, how many women have you been with?

I closed my eyes. So many women's faces appeared. I opened them and said. "I never counted. And you how many men have you been with?"

She said, "Eight men."

"Do you mean eighty?"

She laughed.

I realized something at that moment. A woman will never tell you how many men she's slept with. If she says five, you have to add a zero, or double the number. Because a woman would never give you the correct answer, unless she really wants you to know.

Claudia said, "Ken, have you had any one-night stands?"

I smiled. "Yes, one."

"Describe it," she said.

I closed my eyes to think back. I remembered when I went to Havana, Cuba. It was an amazing city. Vegas had nothing compared to Havana. I was in a casino playing blackjack. I was losing, so I left the table and walked to an elevator.

Before I reached the elevator, an exceptionally beautiful woman with jet-black hair and exquisite black eyes grabbed my hand and said, "I think you are a very attractive man." Then she took my hand and said, "Come with me. You are just the man I'm looking for."

I was shocked. But I followed her to the nearest elevator. Once inside, she pressed against me, kissed me long and hard, and grabbed me.

I wasn't in the mood. I was still trying to figure out what was going on. "Are you selling it?" I asked.

"Are you serious? No, I'm not selling it." Then she proceeded to remove her dress.

I said "Hold it. I don't want you to do that."

"You've got a problem," she said.

Yes, I thought I had a problem.

"What is it?" she asked disinterestedly, zipping up the soft leather dress she had been about to step out of.

May as well end this scene fast.

I stared at her in amazement. I did not believe what was happening. Here was this woman, this strikingly beautiful woman, coming on to me. And she expected instant action. What did she think I was—a traveling man with no feelings? Even though this was new to me, and I didn't care if she was the most gorgeous woman in the world, sex with no communication or conversation was just not for me. I wasn't sixteen and desperate to get laid.

I told her, "My problem is I don't even know your name, let alone what's going on."

"Oh, and if I tell you my name, will that make everything all right?" She mocked me, all zipped up and ready to leave.

"You know what I mean," I said angrily.

"No. I don't know what you mean." She strolled toward the door. "It's simple really. I saw you. I liked you. I thought that maybe the two of us might equal great sex. Obviously, I was wrong. Look," she said impatiently, her hand on the doorknob, "I'm sure we have all made mistakes before. Why don't we just forget the whole thing?"

I have been through a lot of women in my life. But this one took the prize. How could I let her walk out when she was offering a trip I would probably never forget?

I decided to add a little charm to my act. So I said, "I think that maybe we should start from page one. Let's go downstairs, find a bar, have a drink, and get to know each other. Hey, let's at least exchange names. And then, beautiful lady, we can have really great sex. What do you say?"

She looked at me. "That's not a bad idea. You go down to the bar and order me a tequila on the rocks. I want to freshen up." She smiled. "Ten minutes, okay?"

I went down to the bar and ordered her drink. I got myself a grey goose and waited. I glanced at my watch; forty-five minutes had passed. And I realized she obviously had no intention of showing up. Then it came to me; I blew it. She was just a woman who wanted sex from a random guy at that moment. And I blew it.

You can never understand a woman sometimes. I had turned down a great experience. What can I say?

Claudia said, "You mean you turned her down."

"Story of my life," I said.

"So what happened?"

"Four weeks ago, I went to San Juan. I was wandering off down the beach, admiring the scenery. Most of the women wore only the bottom half of scanty bikinis and acted as if they were fully clothed, lying back with open thighs to obtain the perfect tan.

"And then I spotted the girl with the jet-black hair and black eyes who had come on to me in Havana, Cuba. There she was two years later, lying on the beach in San Juan, looking as sensual and wild as ever. Naturally, she was not topless. Why give a free show? She wore a dangerous white bikini and earphones, and her eyes were closed. I recognized her immediately; somehow, she'd made an indelible impression.

"She had one of the horniest bodies I had ever seen. She was tall and slim, with long legs, a small waist, great breasts, and broad shoulders.

"I remembered her walk—panther-like, graceful. I also remembered our one kiss before I had blown the whole thing.

"How was I to approach her now? Why was I going to approach her now? 'You have Andeshia now,' said my conscience sternly.

"'So what?' replied my body temperature.

"'Go ahead.' My body reacted.

"She must have sensed someone staring at her. Without warning, she suddenly sat up, removed the earphones, took off her shades, and returned my quizzical stare."

19

I wasn't close enough to say anything fortunately. Because whenever I opened my mouth, she shot me down.

Did she remember me? Was she going to come over? I stood by the seashore, waiting.

Slowly, she got up, stretched languorously, and headed toward me.

I held my breath; I wasn't single, but I wasn't dead. This was one opportunity I wasn't going to miss, not the second time around.

Our eyes locked. As she got closer, I was mesmerized by the blackness of her eyes, the long lashes that surrounded them, her glowing skin, and her full, lush lips.

I started to say something; I wasn't sure what. "Hello. You again." Something innocuous. It didn't matter. She walked straight past me into the sea.

For a moment, I was stunned, shocked. But my recovery was rapid.

I turned around and watched her stride toward the ocean. She jumped into the ocean toward a floating wooden platform. Without another thought, I took my shirt off, threw it on the sand, and plunged into the sea after her.

She was a powerful swimmer and had a good lead on me. But with my highly personal skills, I set off like a piston and caught up before she was halfway there. I swam alongside her. She didn't say anything. Neither did I.

It was late in the afternoon, and the raft ahead of us looked deserted. I noticed her ears were pierced as her head rose and vanished beneath the surface of the ocean. She wore small diamond earrings. I noticed her arms were strong and powerful as they cleaved the water.

I sensed adventure, knew anything was possible, and didn't draw back. She was amazing.

The funny thing was that she was enjoying the game. She had watched me approach, remembered me from our abortive meeting in Cuba, and wondered whether maybe this was what she needed—a purely physical encounter with no entanglements. If I didn't back off like last time.

She remembered me. Why not put me to the test? After all, fate placed us both on San Juan beach.

She rose and strolled casually toward me. I mumbled something as she passed. She ignored me and plunged into the ocean, knowing I would follow.

We reached the raft together and hauled ourselves aboard. I caught her silent message and didn't say word. The sun was low in the sky, and the people on the beach were beginning to pack up and go home.

Our eyes met, and as if by unspoken agreement, we moved closer. She was staring at me with those crazy black, sensuous gypsy eyes. The signal was clear.

I wanted to know who she was and what was she doing there. Everything about her intrigued me. But the timing was wrong, and I knew it, although that didn't mean I couldn't go along with this game.

I reached out and pulled her to me. She moved into my embrace as naturally as if we had known each other for years. Electricity sparked as we began to kiss, long, lingering kisses with our tongues entwined. Our bodies were wet. I pressed my hands into the small arch of her back and let her feel my hardness. She didn't draw away, but she moved her hips slowly, suggestively. I ran my hands leisurely up her spine, feeling for the ends of her hair. I removed the rubber band and let her hair fall lose to her back.

And while our lips were together, I held her tightly, expertly opened the clasp on her bikini top, let it drop, and felt the excitement of her bare breasts against my chest.

She trailed her hands very slowly down my back, tracing patterns with her fingers, and when she reached the waistband of my pants, she put her hands inside my pants and grabbed me. I moaned, stepped back for a moment, and took my pants off. I didn't care if I was seen from the beach. I didn't care about anything at all, except this crazy real-life fantasy.

Her hands were on me, caressing, stroking, and driving me insane.

"Control," a voice screamed in my head. "Don't blow it."

I reached for her breasts. Hard nipples, soft firm, beautiful, and perfect.

I peeled the bottom of her bikini down, and she stepped out of it. We sank onto the cold surface of the raft, neither of us noticing the discomfort. There was nothing awkward about our lovemaking. I entered her slowly, and she wrapped her long legs tightly around my waist and moved with me as if we had been together many times before. Instinctively, she knew my rhythm, and I knew hers.

As waves were crashing into the shore, I was iron hard but only surfing. The perfect wave had yet to arrive, and when it did, I wanted us to ride it together.

She closed her eyes and gave herself up to the moment. She had known when she first saw me that I would be a sensational lover. And I was. And it frightened her because this was supposed to be a mindless thing, and yet it was more, much more. It was body talk at its most eloquent, and the last thing she needed in her life was another relationship.

She felt it. Her nails dug into me. "Oh God!" she cried out.

And she was lost in sensation, floating in paradise, and taken over by a throbbing release that sent her into spasms of delight.

I felt the same way. The intensity and depth of my orgasm took me by surprise, leaving me shaken and drained. I lay on top of her for a moment, still inside her, and stared into her eyes, which were so deep and full of secrets.

Who was she? I had to know. And yet, she was a woman of mystery. What was I going to say?

I rolled off her, got my pants, and put them on.

She sat up, reached for her bikini, and put it on. She bent forward, shook out her hair, and casually knotted it on top of her head. She looked at me, came close, kissed me, and jumped into the water again. I was speechless; I waited for five minutes, and I followed. By the time I reached the beach, she was gone. And I realized I might never see her again.

20

Andeshia came to my house and banged on my door. "Ken, where have you been? I called you over five times. Or is there a new woman? Knowing you, I wouldn't be surprised."

"Excuse me?" I said.

She stood on my balcony, smoked a cigarette, and then flicked it over the edge. Without another word, as if by mutual agreement, we fell into each other's arms as through it was the most natural thing in the world.

She kissed me with her lips and her tongue, and her hands caressed my face, then moved down to my body with indecent haste.

I returned her kisses, slipped my hands beneath her white dress, and freed her breast. "I want you," I said.

Weakly, she tried to push me away. But I awakened feelings in her that had been long dormant. Sexually, I turned her on to a degree she had forgotten existed. I was a dangerous ride, and she couldn't stop herself.

"Stop teasing me," I said.

"I never tease," she said, unzipping my pants and sinking to her knees. "Never." And her mouth was on me, taking me to heaven and back and swallowing the evidence.

"God." I had experienced the good, the bad, and the ugly of sex. But I had never experienced sex as erotic and exciting as with Andeshia. I came to understand something: falling in love is like getting hit by a truck and yet not being mortally wounded. You're just sick to your stomach, high one moment and low the next. You're starving hungry but unable to eat. You're full of hope and enthusiasm.

It's also being unable to remove the smile from your face. You love life with a mad, passionate intensity and feel ten years younger.

Love doesn't appear with any warning signs. You fall into it as if pushed from a high roller coaster.

There's no time to think about what's happening. It's inevitable.

21

I have being running scared all my life, looking for that one woman. I've met so many, but I was still looking for that one, the one that would fulfill my very being. But most women wanted something greater than them. They were confused in every sense of the word. Don't get me wrong; I met awesome women. But they weren't serious. This is why you can never underestimate a woman. They have ways of doing things, telling lies, and deceiving you. It's amazing sometimes; that's why nothing a woman ever does surprises me.

I'm never shocked anymore, never surprised. I'm just disappointed.

There was Erika Douglas from Trenton, New Jersey. She was an awesome woman. But she didn't know what she wanted. She actually told me this.

I have two daughters from two different fathers. Are you ready for me? Tried to make me feel guilty. Told me I'm hindering her from doing what she had to do; we had an awesome time together. We laughed about everything. Then the day we made love.

One lovely evening. The next day, she called at exactly 12:55 a.m. and said, "I can't see you anymore. I have to stop talking to you."

I wasn't shocked, just disappointed because I'd expected more from her.

The attraction died in that moment. Then she stopped calling; she was waiting for me to call. Making excuses. I liked her a lot. I fell for her. I would have given her the world if she had asked me to.

I thought she was the one. But her mind was elsewhere. Deep down, she didn't know what she wanted. My guess was she was looking for something that wasn't there. Maybe a rich guy or something. Who knows. She was running, but no one was chasing her. She changed her men like she changed clothes.

I tried to show her something different. But she was way gone. She wasn't looking for love, just excitement. She wanted to have fun and play the field. I was furious about why. It was her life. She would learn.

Are there any girls that aren't about games? To know women, you will have to think like them. After you lose something, you realize it's serious.

But women would never understand their actions.

There was Leshanna Csikortos. She was an amazing woman. She was married to a white man in the army. She had his son and had another daughter by a different guy. But she fell in love with me. Thought she did.

But she was an incredible liar. I mean, she flew me to Chicago, and we had an awesome time together. She came to New York and stayed with me for a week. But she was still married. She got pregnant and swore to God and man that it was mine. But you can't love two men. She lived with her husband in Washington State. And she dated me in New York. Didn't question her. So she said she was pregnant and it was mine.

Then three months down the line, she called me crying, saying she'd had a miscarriage. She had been in the hospital for three days. I was shocked. I asked what had happened. She said she didn't know. How could I question her? She even gave me the hospital's name and the doctor's name that did her miscarriage.

She was bluntly lying to me about everything. I mean, she was good. But being fake and pretending is not a way of life. Lying about a man's child is the lowest thing a woman can ever do.

I mean, she cried on the phone. She fooled me. All along, she was lying.

Then she broke up with me through a text. I wasn't surprised. I didn't question her. I didn't reply to her. She was devastated and shocked. Her game didn't work.

Then she found out somehow how about Andeshia. But I was in Europe. She called and said she was still pregnant and started sending me ultrasounds and pictures of herself. And everything showed me that she was still pregnant and that she had divorced her husband for me. And she wished things could work out. She was just a woman based on lies. But she was still pregnant. And she said I was the father.

But she was another confused woman without a plan. Deep down, she didn't know what she wanted. All she wanted was someone to father her kids, a good man. But she would never be a faithful woman for any man nor a good wife. She was very deceitful.

I would have given her a chance. But the damage was done.

She lied beyond reasonable doubt. She was conniving. She looked at me and said her husband was better than I was.

I smiled and didn't argue; I didn't get mad. What would have been the use? She didn't know what she wanted. But she asked herself why she was alone and why she felt lonely.

So the conception of women is easy. There are good women and bad ones. There are conniving ones. It's up to you to find the real ones.

There was Tracy Marie from eastern New York; she was an awesome woman. She asked me to marry her. I told her not yet. I needed to be established. But she left me and started dating a black cop. And even while she was with that man, she still kept coming to see me and bringing me Chinese food at all hours of the night. She knew I loved Chinese food. Then we would just sit in her car and talk for hours.

"I still want you, Ken," she said.

"How?" I said. "You live with this black cop now."

"Make up your mind, Tracy," I said.

So she left. She stayed with the black cop.

She thought he was the man for her. She got pregnant by him and had a gorgeous daughter.

But she still felt alone, and she wondered why. Deep down, she was lonely and miserable without reason.

I mean, she met my mother, which I consider a privilege. But she was looking for something that wasn't there.

To this day, she still calls me. We had something that has never been forgotten. But she is the one going through the heartache and pain.

Then there was Christine Hufford from Pennsylvania; she lived in New Jersey and was an amazing woman with contingencies. She was different; she was a brunette with an amazing figure. She was my escape, my dream, and my vision. I had her dye her hair black for me, which made her drop-dead gorgeous. But she suffered from the same diseases—deceitfulness and trust issues, and they ruined us. I woke up night after night to see her going through my phone, looking for something that wasn't there. Then she'd fight me because I woke up and caught her. She was lost. The attraction died. What we had died.

These are just the acts of women I encountered.

But these women will never find happiness since they will date more men. But they'll still feel alone. It's like throwing stones in a quiet pool. There is no happiness for women who think their greatest worth is in bed.

I'm the one man that had dated them and knew who they were and knew deep down inside what they really wanted.

It's amazing, but it's the story of my life. I mean, every woman I've ever been with had a part of me. But somehow, somewhere, there always seemed to crush it and kill it for some unknown reason. What can I say?

People ask me why I always look angry and mad. Why wouldn't I? What's to laugh about?

I can't complain; my life hasn't been good so far. Life has made me good.

My mum always said to me, "Good looks are not going to get you places. You have to be the fastest and smartest in business, and you have to know how to treat a woman in bed. That way, you will have the world by its balls. Believe me, that's what makes a man."

Being successful in life isn't just about working hard; it's about working smarter and knowing what's going to happen before it happens.

I thought I have found the woman that it's so special because I have been playing the games of women for so long I don't think I have a heart anymore.

I came to understand attraction isn't a choice. It has to be perceived. If a woman is not attracted to you, I don't care if you give her a million dollars, she is not attracted to you.

Nothing will make her, not even money. Just as any man can make a baby with any woman, the point is not making a baby. It's who you make the baby with that matters.

It's America. What can I say? I learned that to be successful, you need friends. To be very successful, you need enemies. But never betray your friends or the people who love you. Cardinal rule. Law of the universe. A thousand more crimes have been committed in the name of love than in the name of hate.

22

It's four in the morning. And I wipe the sleep from my eyes; I'm lying down with my eyes closed, thinking about my life, women, and my family. It's hectic.

My phone rings. I stare at the phone for five minutes, watching it ring and ring and asking myself who in the hell is calling this early. My head is pounding. There's so much on my mind. But the phone keeps ringing, breaking my train of thoughts.

I snatch the phone from the receiver. "Hello."

"I hate men."

"Hello."

"Why is life so cruel?"

"Who is this?"

"It's your sister Penny."

"Hey, sis."

"Why are men so devious?"

But all the same.

"They're still devious." Show me a beautiful woman, and I will show you a man that is tired of sleeping with her.

"What's wrong, sis? Talk to me. Where are you?"

"Venice, Italy."

"Jesus, what are you doing over there?"

"You know we both have this indescribable need to see the world. And when you left for New York, I came here. The history, beauty, and romance of Italy is remarkable."

"So, what happened? Why do you feel terrible?" I said.

"Just listen. I went to Finland for three days with a friend, and then I ended up in Italy. I arrived at seven in the evening. The city was magnificent. It was like watching a full moon on a remarkable evening in Venice. I felt like heaven, but I had nowhere to go.

"I knew no one, not a soul. I felt lost. But still, I was drawn in by the city's beauty. I walked the streets of Venice hour after hour. I checked into a hotel with all the money I had. I left my bag in the hotel room and walked out. I felt lost.

"I just kept walking, admiring and stopping at every shop to gaze at the incredible displays of jewelry and dresses and leather goods and perfumes.

"I started feeling tired and hungry. And I had no money on me. And since I had no money on me at all, I had to find a way to survive until I could find a job the next day.

"To solve my immediate problem, I needed to find someone to buy me a good hot dinner.

"I asked directions to an expensive hotel. This guy told me about Hotel Danieli, which is located in one of the most prestigious positions in Venice, just a few steps from Saint Mark's square, looking out over the lagoon and its myriad of islands. The hotel's setting is so close to Piazza San Marco, conveniently located next to shopping areas, museums, outdoor cafés, and the most interesting attractions Venice has to offer.

"I was impressed. So I went there. When I got inside, the lobby was a masterpiece of subdued elegance, soft and understated.

"I walked in confidently, as if I belonged there, and took a seat in a chair facing the elevator. I had never done this before, and I was bit nervous. But I remembered how easy it was when I saw beautiful women do it in movies.

"Men are really not very complicated. There's only one lesson a girl has to remember: a man is soft when he is hard and hard when he is soft. So, it's only necessary to keep him hard until he's given you what you wanted.

"Now, looking around the lobby, I decided that it would be a simple matter to catch the eye of an unattached male on his way, perhaps, to a lonely dinner."

"So what happened?" I said.

"'Excuse me, Miss,' a man said with a deep Italian accent.

"I turned my head to look up at a large man in a dark suit. I had never seen a detective in my life, but there was no doubt whatever in my mind.

"'Are you waiting for someone?'

"'Yes,' I replied, trying to keep my voice steady. 'I'm waiting for a friend.'

"I was suddenly acutely aware of my wrinkled dress and the fact that I wasn't carrying my purse.

"'Is your friend a guest of this hotel?'

"I felt a surge of panic rising in me. 'He…is not exactly.'

"He studied me for a minute and then said in a hardened tone, 'May I see your identification?'

"'I…I don't have it with me,' I stammered. 'I lost it.'

"The detective said, 'Perhaps you will come with me.' He put a firm hand on my arm, and I rose to my feet.

"And at that moment, someone took my other arm and said, 'Sorry I'm late, *cherie*, but you know how those damned cocktail parties are. You have to blast your way out. Been waiting long?'

"I swung around in astonishment to look at the speaker. He was a tall man; his body was lean and hard looking, and he was outrageously attractive. He had long black hair with a widow's peak and eyes the color of a dark, stormy sea, with long thick lashes. He had an irregular face; it was a face that was extraordinarily alive and mobile so that you felt it was ready to smile, to laugh, or to frown. The only thing that saved it from being femininely beautiful was a strong masculine chin with a deep cleft in it.

"He gestured toward the detective. 'Is this man bothering you?' His voice was deep, and he spoke Italian with a very slight accent.

"'N…no,' I said in a bewildered voice.

"'I beg your pardon, sir,' the hotel detective was saying. 'I misunderstood. We have been having a problem here lately with…' He turned to me. 'Please accept my apologies, Miss.'

"The stranger turned to me. 'Well now, I don't know. What do you think?'

"I swallowed and nodded quickly.

"The man turned to the detective. 'My lady is being generous. Just watch yourself in the future.' He took my arm and then headed for the door.

"When we reached the street, I said, 'I…I don't know how to thank you. Mr…'

"'I have always hated policemen.' The stranger grinned. 'Do you want me get you a taxi?'

"I stared at him, and the panic began to rise in me again as I remembered my situation. 'No.'

"'Right. Good night.' He walked over to the stand and started to get into a taxi, turned around, and saw that I was standing there, rooted, staring after him.

"In the doorway of the hotel, the detective was watching.

"The stranger hesitated and then walked back to me.

"'You'd better get out of here,' he advised. 'Our friend is still interested in you.'

"'I have nowhere to go,' I said.

"He nodded and reached into his pocket.

"'I don't want your money,' I said quickly.

"He looked at me in surprise. 'What do you want?'

"'To have dinner with you.'

"He smiled and said, 'Sorry. I have a date, and I'm late already.'

"'Then go ahead,' I said. 'I will be fine.'

"He shoved the bills back into his pocket. 'Suit yourself, honey,' he said. '*Au 'voir.*' He turned and began walking toward the taxi again.

"I looked after him, wondering what was wrong with me. I knew I had behaved stupidly, but I also knew that I could not have done anything else. From the first moment I had looked at him, I had experienced a reaction that I had never felt before, a wave of emotion so strong that I could almost reach out and touch it. And I didn't even know his name and would probably never see him again. I glanced toward the hotel and saw the detective moving purposefully toward me. It was my own fault. This time, she would not be able to talk her way out of it.

"I felt a hand on my shoulder, and as I turned to see who it was, the stranger took my arm and propelled me toward the taxi, quickly opened the door, and climbed in beside me. He gave the driver an address. The taxi pulled away, leaving the detective at the curb, staring after us.

"'What about your date?' I asked.

"'It's a party.' He shrugged. 'One more won't make any difference. I'm Novilari Reed. What's your name?'

"'Penny Lope Madu.'

"'Where are you from, Penny?'

"I turned and looked into his brilliant dark eyes and said, 'Amsterdam. I am the daughter of a prince.'

"He laughed, showing even white teeth.

"'Good for you, Princess,' he said.

"'Are you English?' I said.

"'American,' he said.

"So the stranger talked about himself. I didn't care about what he was saying; I just enjoyed watching his face as he talked. His dark eyes sparkled with enthusiasm as he spoke, blazing with an overpowering, irresistible vitality.

"I had never met anyone like him. He was that rarity or rarities—a spendthrift with himself. He was open and warm and alive, sharing himself, enjoying life, and making sure that everyone around him enjoyed it too. He was like a magnet, pulling everyone who approached into his orbit.

"We arrived at the party, which was being given in a small flat in downtown Venice. The apartment was filled with a group of laughing, shouting people, most of whom were young. Novilari introduced me to the hostess, a predatory, sexy-looking woman. And then was swallowed by the crowd. I caught glimpses of him during the evening surrounded by eager young girls, each trying to capture his attention. And yet, there was no ego about him, I thought. It was as though he were totally unaware of how attractive he was.

"Someone found a drink for me, and someone else offered to bring me a plate of food from the buffet. But I was suddenly not hungry. I wanted to be with the American, wanted to get him away from the girls who crowded around him. Men were coming up to me and trying to start conversations, but my mind was elsewhere. From the moment we walked in, the American had completely ignored me, had acted as though I did not exist. 'Why not?' I thought.

"Why would he bother with me when he could have any girl at the party?

"Two men were trying to engage me in conversation, but I could not concentrate. The room had suddenly become unbearably hot. I looked around for a means of escape.

"A voice said in my ear, 'Let's go,' and a few moments, later the American and I were out on the street, in the cool night air. The city was dark and quiet against the invisible clouds in the sky. And the cars glided through the street like silent fish in a black sea. We could not find a taxi, so we walked and had dinner in a little restaurant, and I found out that I was starved. I studied the American sitting across from me, and I wondered what it was that had happened to me.

"It was as though he had touched some wellspring deep within me that I had never known existed. I had never felt happiness like that before. His words were very articulate, like stones in a quiet pool. We talked about everything; I told him about my background, and he told me that he was from Manhattan, New York.

"'Where did you learn to speak Italian so well?' I asked.

"'I used to spend my summers in Rome, Italy when I was a kid. My old man was a stock-market tycoon.'

"So, he was explaining to me the ways of the stock market in America. I did not care what he talked about, so long as he kept talking.

"'Where are you living?' he asked me.

"'Nowhere.' I told him I'd just flown in. He laughed.

"That night, I moved in with Novilari at a small exquisite hotel. There was no discussion about it.

"It was inevitable for both of us. When we made love that night, it was more exciting than anything I had ever known. It was a wild, primitive explosion that shook us both. I lay in Novilari's arms all night, holding him close, happier than I had ever dreamed possible.

"The next morning, we awoke and made love. He aroused me to heights of passion I had not felt in years.

"I told him to lie still. I began to experiment on him with my tongue and my mouth and my hands, trying new things, finding the soft sensitive areas of his body and working on them until he cried aloud with pleasure.

"We went out to explore the city. Novilari was a wonderful guide. And he made Venice seem like a lovely toy for my amusement. We had lunch and spent the afternoon just walking and talking. I was lost in his words. He took me to an exquisite restaurant where we had dinner. And we just spent hours wandering the city of Italy. I mean, Venice was beautiful beyond sight, and we both finished up by having onion soup at four in the morning. I had made a lot of friends, and I realized that the stranger Novilari had a gift of laughter. He taught me to laugh, and I had not known that laughter was within me. It was a gift from God. I was grateful to Novilari and very much in love with him. It was dawn when we returned to the hotel room. I was exhausted, but Novilari was filled with energy, a restless dynamo. I lay in bed watching him as he stood at the window looking at the sun rise over the rooftops of Italy.

"'I love Venice, Italy,' he said. 'It's like a temple to the best things that men have ever done. It's a city of beauty and food and love.' He turned to me and grinned. 'Not necessarily in that order.'

"I watched as he took off his clothes and climbed into bed beside me. I held him, loving the feel of him and the male smell of him. I knew now that they were men like Novilari Reed. And I also knew that there could never be anyone else for me.

"'Do you know who the two greatest men who ever lived were, Princess?' he asked.

"'You,' I said.

"He laughed. And later said casually, 'Why don't we get married?'

"It was the happiest moment of my life.

"Saturday was a relaxed, lazy day. We had breakfast at a little outdoor café and went back to the room and spent almost the entire day in bed. I could not believe anyone could be so ecstatic. It was pure magic when we made love. But I was just as content to lie there, listen to Novilari talk and watch him as he moved restlessly about the room. Just being near him was enough for me. It was odd, I thought, how things worked. 'When I am with Novilari, I am something.' He had restored my faith in men. He was my world. And I knew that I would never need anything more, and it seemed incredible to me that I could be so lucky, that he felt the same way about me.

"'I was never going to get married,' he said. 'But to hell with that. Plans are made to be changed, right, Princess?'

"I nodded, filled with a happiness that threatened to burst inside me.

"'Let's get married by some priest in the country,' he said. 'Unless you want a big wedding.'

"I shook my head. 'The country sounds wonderful.'

"He nodded. 'Deal. I have to go to report back to England tonight. I will meet you here next Friday. How does that sound?'

"'I…I don't know if I can stand being away from you that long.' My voice was shaky.

"Novilari took me in his arms and held me. 'Do you love me?' he asked.

"'More than my life,' I replied simply.

"Four hours later, Novilari was on his way back to England. He did not let me drive to the airport with him.

"'I don't like good-byes,' he said, and he gave me a large fistful of euros. 'Buy yourself a wedding gown, Princess. I will see you in it next week.' And he was gone.

"I spent the next week in a state of euphoria, going back to the places Novilari and I had been. I spent hours dreaming about our life together.

"The days seemed to drag by. The minutes stubbornly refused to move until I thought I would go out of my mind. I went to a dozen shops looking for a wedding dress. And finally, I found exactly what I wanted at a Gucci store. It was a beautiful white organza dress with a high-necked bodice, long sleeves, a row of six pearl buttons, and three crinoline petticoats. It cost much more than I had anticipated. But I did not hesitate. I used all the money that Novilari had given me and nearly all of my own savings. My whole being was centered on Novilari. I thought about ways to please him. I searched through my mind for memories that might amuse him and anecdotes that would entertain him. I felt like a schoolgirl.

"And so it was that I waited for Friday to come. I was in an agony of impatience, and when it finally arrived, I was up at dawn and spent two hours bathing and dressing, changing clothes and changing again, trying to guess which dress would please Novilari most. I put on my wedding gown. But I quickly took it off again, afraid that it might bring bad luck. I was in a frenzy of excitement.

"At eleven o' clock, I stood in front of the pier glass in the bedroom, and I knew that I had never looked as beautiful as I did then. There was no ego in my appraisal: I was simply pleased for Novilari. I was glad that I could bring him this gift. By noon, he had not appeared. And I wished that he had told me what time he expected to arrive. I kept phoning the desk for messages every ten minutes and kept picking up the phone to make sure it was working. By seven that evening, there was still no word from him.

"By midnight, he had not called. And I sat huddled in a chair, staring at the phone and willing it to ring.

"I fell asleep, and when I woke, it was dawn. It was Saturday, and I was still in the chair. I was stiff and cold. The dress I had so carefully chosen was wrinkled, and there was a run in my stocking.

"I changed clothes and stayed in the room all that day, stationing myself in front of the open window, and telling myself that if I stayed there, Novilari would appear but if I left, something terrible would happen to him. As Saturday morning lengthened into afternoon, I began to be filled with the conviction that there had been an accident. Novilari's plane had crashed, and he was lying in a field or in a hospital, wounded or dead. My mind was filled with ghastly visions. I sat up all night on Saturday, sick with worry, afraid to leave the room, and not knowing how to reach Novilari.

"When I had not heard from him by Sunday at noon, I could stand it no longer. I had to telephone him. But how? It was difficult to place an overseas call, and I was not even certain where Novilari was. I knew he worked in a British company. I picked up the phone and spoke to a switchboard operator.

"'It is impossible,' the operator said flatly.

"I explained the situation, and whether it was my words or the frantic despair in my voice I never knew, but three hours later, I was talking to a representative from the British company. They could not help me, but they transferred me to a different person who put me through to Operations, where I was disconnected before I could get any information. It was six more hours before I was reconnected, and by then, I was on the verge of hysteria. Operations could give me no information and suggested I try again.

"'I have talked to them!" I screamed into the phone. I began to sob.

"The male English voice at the other end of the phone said in embarrassment, 'Please, Miss, it can't be that bad. Hold on a moment.'

"I held the receiver in my hand, knowing that it was hopeless and certain that Novilari was dead and that I would never know how or where he died. And I was about to replace the receiver when the voice spoke in my ear again and said cheerfully, 'Who are you?'

"'I'm his fiancée.'

"For a miraculous instant, the line cleared, and the voice said, 'Novilari Reed is on weekend leave. If it's urgent, he can be reached at the Hotel Savoy in London.' And the line went dead.

"When the maid came to clean the room the next morning, she found me on the floor, semiconscious. The maid stared at me for a moment, tempted to mind her own business and leave. She came over and touched my forehead. I was burning hot. Grumbling, the maid waddled down the hall and asked the porter to send up the manager. Twenty minutes later, an ambulance pulled up outside the hotel, and three young interns carrying a stretcher were directed to my room.

"I was unconscious. The young intern in charge raised my eyelids, put a stethoscope to my chest, and listened to the rales as I breathed. I had a high fever.

"Pneumonia.

"'Let's get her out of here.' They lifted me onto the stretcher, and three minutes later, the ambulance was racing toward the hospital. I was rushed into an oxygen tent. And it was six days later before I was fully conscious. I dragged myself reluctantly up from the green depths of oblivion. Subconsciously, I knew something terrible had happened, and I was fighting not to remember what it was.

"As the awful thing floated closer and closer to the surface of my mind, I struggled to keep it from myself. It suddenly became clear and whole. Novilari Reed. I began to weep until I finally drifted off into a half sleep.

"I felt a hand gently holding me. And I knew Novilari had come back to me and that everything was all right. I opened my eyes and stared at a stranger in a white uniform who was taking my pulse.

"'Well, welcome back,' he said.

"'Where am I?' I asked.

"'In the municipal hospital in the Cannaregio District,' he said.

"'What am I doing here?'

"'Getting well. You have had pneumonia. I'm Dr. Stone.' He was young, with deep-set dark eyes.

"'Are you my doctor?'

"'Yes. I'm glad you made it; I wasn't sure you would survive.'

"'How long have I been here?'

"'Six days.'

"'Would you do me a favor?" I asked weakly.

"'If I can.'

"'Call the hotel that brought me here and ask them...' I hesitated. 'Ask them if there are any messages for me.'

"'Well, I'm awfully busy...'

"I squeezed his hands fiercely. 'Please. It's important. My fiancé is trying to get in touch with me.'

"He grinned. 'I don't blame him. All right, I will take care of it,' he promised. 'Now get some sleep.'

"'Not until I hear from you,' I said.

"He left, and I lay down to wait. Of course, Novilari had been trying to get in touch with me. There had been some terrible misunderstanding. He would explain it all to me, and everything would be fine again.

"It was four hours before the doctor returned. He walked up to my bed and set down two suitcases. 'I brought you your clothes. I went to the hotel myself,' he said.

"I looked up at him.

"'I'm sorry,' he said, embarrassed. 'There were no messages.'

"I stared at him for a long time. It all came to me in a flash. Novilari had played me, lied to me, betrayed me, and deceived me.

"I was released from the hospital three days later. Dr. Stone came to say good-bye to me. 'Do you have any place to go?' he asked. 'Or a job?'

"I said, 'No. I don't need your help. Thank you.'

"I went to a small street café and sat down, sipping coffee and deciding how to pick up the pieces of my life. I knew I had to survive, for I had a reason to live now. I was filled with a deep and burning hatred that was so all consuming that it left no room for anything or anyone else.

"I was avenging and rising from the ashes of the emotions that Novilari Reed had murdered in me. I would not rest until I destroyed him. He killed a part of me.

"It seemed to me that I had died and been born again. Slowly, I had become aware of my surroundings. I was filled with a hatred such as I had not known could exist.

"The first thing I did when I unpacked in a small hotel room I had rented was to hang up my wedding dress. I put it in the front of the closet so that it was the first thing I saw in the morning and the last thing I saw when I undressed at night in order to remember his betrayal.

"Because the end of my life had happened, and everything I believed in had died—my faith, my hope, my laughter, and my joy. My future had died in that moment. My pain was deeper than tears."

23

"Hello? Hello? Brother, are you still there?"

"Yes, I'm here, sis." I had been on the phone with my sister for nine hours straight, listening to her story about what had happened to her in Venice, Italy, and the reasons she hated men and despised them. "Hello?"

"Brother? Hello?"

"I'm here, sis. I'm here."

"I'm here telling you my pain. And you are not even listening."

"I'm all ears, sis. I heard every word you said…I'm just shocked, speechless. Sis, talk to me. What do you want done?"

"Brother, I want a first-class ticket to New York. Now. And I want you to be at the airport. Your presence is required, not requested."

"I will be there, Sister. I will get your ticket for you in an hour. You should be able to go to the airport, and it will be there. I will put it for tomorrow afternoon. I will pick you up at six, when the plane arrives, if there aren't any delays. Ok, sis?

"One more thing, Brother."

"Yes."

"I'm pregnant."

"What?"

"I knew I was pregnant before there were any visible signs of it, before taking any tests, before I missed my period. I could sense the new life that had formed in my womb. And at night, I lay in bed staring at the ceiling and thinking about it."

"So you haven't had any tests done?" I said.

"I don't need any tests. You know me, Brother. A woman knows her body. And I know mine, inside and out."

"Okay, Sister. I'll get you a pregnancy test when you get here."

"I will see you tomorrow."

"Have a safe flight."

"Bye."

"I love you, Brother."

"I love you, sis."

"Bye."

"Bye."

24

Love is a language. It's tragic when you lose it.

I came to understand that; never lie to a woman.

The key to a woman's heart is an unexpected gift at an unexpected time.

I learned that if you ever want to have an affair with a public figure, do it in the open. Take her to public places, well-known restaurants, and theaters. For people are always looking for devious motives. They will say to themselves, "He is taking so-and-so out in public. I wonder who he is seeing secretly." People never believe the obvious.

Attraction isn't logical. Attraction is a very powerful emotion that has reason. Once any woman is attracted to you, it doesn't matter if you are a bastard or are abusive. She will still be with you. For that strong feeling that she feels about you. Which is that she is extremely attracted to you.

I sat there, thinking. I had an interview in the morning. I had to pick my sister up at six. And I was still stunned and playing my sister's story in my mind.

I decided to stay in that day and just sleep and think.

My interview was at noon. I woke up at ten the next morning. I was very grumpy and tired. I got dressed. I wore a black silk suit and black shoes. I shaved. I was looking very well dressed. I got into my car and drove into Manhattan.

I was hungry, so I went into a café on Twenty-Third and Sixth Avenue and got a coffee with a danish. I sat down and ate. I was tired, and I still had to go to my interview. I mean, looking for a good job in New York was a headache. You had to know somebody that knew somebody. It was all a chain of command. Because if you didn't know anybody, you were screwed. And again, I think that happens everywhere.

I drank my coffee and thought about the rest of my day: my interview, picking up my sister from the airport, and everything. So I just sat and thought.

There was this picture on the wall in the café—a very magnificent image of a lion roaring and ready to attack. With people around it appalling. I was staring at the picture on the wall. There was something about the image that kept me tuned in.

I was intrigued by the picture on the wall. I was still staring at the image on the wall when a woman walked in with her brother, nephew, son, or cousin; I had no idea who the little guy was.

I mean, she was beyond beautiful. She had to be in her early twenties, with skin the color of melted honey and a face that was a photographer's dream. Her body was made for sin. She had very exquisite long black hair, intelligent soft brown eyes, sensual full lips, lovely long legs, and a figure filled with erotic promise. Her dark hair was cut short in deliberate dishabille, with a few strands sprawling across her forehead. I mean, she was beyond intriguing. One look at her, and I wanted her.

She turned and stared at me for an instant, just a second. Then she turned to go get her coffee. For the first time in my life, I was speechless. I didn't know how to approach this woman, which shocked me. I stared at her, and I knew I had to say something. I got up. I walked up to her, and said, "Excuse me."

She turned and stared at me.

I said, "What's the occasion? You are a vision. You look intriguing—your outfit, the skirt, everything about you."

She smiled and laughed. "No occasion. I'm going to work."

I laughed. "Impressive. I'm Ken. You are?"

"Shantel. Shantel Williams."

"It's my pleasure, Shantel."

"Likewise."

"What do you do, Shantel?"

"I'm a photographer and a retail worker at Best Buy."

"So you love beautiful things."

"Yes, I do."

"So do I."

I stared at the painting on the wall. Death on a pale horse. My favorite image is the lion attacking.

"You."

"I love the whole thing."

"I have an interview to go to..."

"What's your number? I would love to know you."

Shantel took my hand, pulled a pen out of her pocket, wrote her number on my hand, and walked out of the café.

I called her that night and invited her for tea that weekend. A tea date, she is was gamed.

25

I was running late to pick my sister up. By the time I got to JFK Airport, it was crowded. So many people were rushing out, and then, in that moment, I saw my sister. She looked different—radiant, exquisite. She looked up, saw me, and ran to me, and we hugged. I held her for ten minutes, which felt like an eternity.

We walked outside and went to my car. And I drove home. As soon as I got in, Penny walked to the bedroom and fell asleep.

I sat in the living room, consumed by my own thoughts. And I fell into a deep sleep.

I woke up the next morning before my sister woke up, and I went to see Andeshia. Something in me was bugging me to go see her. It hit me after I saw her what it was.

26

Andeshia said, "Look beyond this beautiful face and analyze my mind. Write an analytical essay about the depths of my persuasion, and explain to the people that you've never tasted me, yet you know my flavor." Hmm. I was impressed by this, but what made it more intriguing was that she knew she affected me in a way no woman had done before.

"Hey, Ken," she said.

I smiled. "My beautiful." I gave her a hug. I didn't know why I felt so happy, and then it hit me. One moment can change your mind, one look can change your heart, and one person can change your destiny.

She was wearing blue jeans and white D&G glasses, and her hair was tied up in a ponytail. She had on an exquisite pink jacket with something written on the back of it. None of that mattered because I was just staring at her. I wanted her without having a reason.

"Ken, I'm pregnant..."

"You're what?"

"I'm pregnant."

I closed my eyes for a minute. My whole body shut down. I opened my eyes and my mouth, but the words didn't come out. I finally spoke. "How far long are you?"

"Two months."

"I thought you were on the pill."

"You never asked…I wasn't."

"You have just changed the nature of our relationship."

"Should I be sorry?"

"Not really. But we'd better define what our new relationship is."

"Marry me, Ken. I'm having your baby."

I closed my eyes again, thinking. My sister thought she was pregnant, and now this. "Hun, you are irresistible; you an amazing woman. Give me time. I need to think. This is too much."

"Ok," she said. She came close to me, kissed me, and walked away.

I was shocked. I needed someone to talk to. I called Claudia to see whether she was home. She answered on the first ring. I invited myself over.

She laughed and said, "I'm waiting." She gave me the address.

Andeshia's news about being pregnant depressed me.

I got to Claudia's house in Brooklyn. It was spacious, simple but decent. It was funny as I walked in. She opened the door, and I fell into her arms.

I sat down. She ask me what I wanted to drink.

"Scotch on the rocks, straight."

"Long day."

"No, a complicated day," I said.

She disappeared for twenty minutes.

She came back in a white silk bra and panties with a white shimming scalf around her neck. She walked toward me. My heart was beating fast. I swallowed the scotch in one shot. She moved seductively.

She was in front of me. "Take off your clothes."

It wasn't a statement, and I obliged.

I got up and took my clothes off. And as if by unspoken agreement, we fell into each other's arms and made passionate love over and over again.

I got up, went to the fridge, drank some water, and took some frozen pineapple slices from the freezer. I brought them back to her and fed her the pineapples with a fork.

Claudia stared at me while I fed her. I stared back at her. There were tears standing like shining diamonds in the corners of her eyes.

"Hun, what's wrong?"

"I love you. You are what I have been waiting for. Stay with me," she said.

I did.

The next morning, I woke up alone. I looked around. No one was there; she had left a note that said, "See you later, sleepyhead. Love you." And signed.

I smiled and lay back in the bed, staring at the ceiling and thinking, "What am I looking for? What do I really want?"

I had to call my best friend and business partner. He always had answers for me when I was stuck. I somehow always kept him updated with anything new in my life and told him about the women I had been seeing. He was the only one who knew me that well.

At that point, Andeshia was pregnant. Claudia might have been. But both of them were madly in love with me. I knew I had to choose one, but which. So I decided to play it out and see what was in the cards for me. I had nothing to lose. They were both amazing women. I just needed to think, set my act straight, and find one woman and stick with her. But not just any woman. I wanted someone who understood me for who I was, without judgment or questions. Someone who didn't care about the past but was ready for the future with me. Someone who was ready and willing to take me as is. And someone who was as ready to give her world to me as I was to her.

I had to call my business partner.

27

I picked my phone up to call my business partner. Jay Vargas had been my business partner since college—same school, same classes, same graduation, same everything. He was the closest thing I had to a brother. When I was in trouble or my chips were down, I could call him, and he would make magic happen.

This time, I needed to talk to him. He always had answers for me.

The phone rang and rang.

"What's happening; it's me."

"Talk to me," Jay said.

"I messed up again; I wasn't thinking. I think I've gotten two girls pregnant. Andeshia is pregnant. And I'm not too sure, but I think Claudia is too. And to top it off, my sister says she is pregnant too."

"This nigga," he says.

"I wasn't thinking. I was living the dream."

"You will have to choose. Who do you want to be with? You can't chase two rats. If you do, you'll lose both."

"I don't know. I'm confused."

"What is this?" he says. "We have businesses to run, things to establish, ideas to create, things to launch, places to travel to, islands to see, resorts to build, and acers to buy. Wake the fuck up. You're making babies. Figure it out. And fast.

"I'm here if you need me. I have been in your shoes. I have been there. I had an experience where I was struggling to deal with being alone, feeling forsaken and betrayed by putting my trust in the wrong person. When you try to prove that you love somebody more than you love yourself, you become unlovable.

"So I need you to think and think fast. There is nothing wrong with having a baby. It's who you have it with that matters.

"I need you to focus," Jay said. "Remember, don't stay with her because she is pregnant. Stay because you want to."

"I got it. I will call you if anything."

"Bye."

"One."

"Bye."

I hung up, contemplating. There was so much to think about; the timing was not right. I closed my eyes, thinking.

My phone started ringing. I picked it up without looking to see who was calling. "Hello."

"Hey, bro."

"Sis."

"I told you."

"What?"

"I'm pregnant."

"How sure are you?"

"Very. I took six pregnancy tests. They all came back positive. I told you I know my body, every inch."

"What's the plan?"

"I'm having it."

"Really."

"Yes, bro. Really."

"Ok. I'm with you all the way. Since we're on that topic, I'm having a baby too, sis."

"What? Since when?"

"I just found out."

"Come meet me. Let's go drinking. I'm depressed."

"Where?"

"On Forty-Fourth and Eighth Avenue. There's a quiet simple Thai place. We need to sit and talk."

An hour later, my sister met me at the Thai place. I was sitting inside when she walked in. I waved to her. She saw me and walked over. We hugged, and she sat.

"I'm starved," she said.

Order.

She got pad thai and a club soda. I just wanted to drink. So I ordered Absolute vodka neat. She ate, and I drank. She said she was ready to have the baby.

"Are you excited? It's a big deal."

"I don't know, bro."

"Would you still go find the dad?"

"Fuck him," she said. "He killed everything female inside me. Bro, he shattered my soul. The pain was unbearable. I never knew love could be so painful. I can't believe one man can make me feel like nothing else matters in this world. I love every bone inside that man."

Tears came down my sister's face like shining stars. The tears just kept falling down her face. I stared at her and didn't know what to say. Watching my sister cry killed my spirit deep down in my soul. I loved her. But to see that a man had damaged her like this broke my spirit.

"Sis, it's okay. It happened. It's time to move on. Everyone gets heartbroken; it's part of life. It's how you pick yourself up that matters. It's time to relive your life. Have the baby. Take a trip. Dye your hair. Do something out the ordinary. And I will back you up all the way."

"Bro, should I go find him? Make him suffer," she said.

"No, sis. It's not worth it. His time will come. I just need you to focus on you. Right now, only you matters. Nothing else."

We ate, drank, and went home. Both of us were consumed by our own thoughts.

28

I figured it was time for some thinking. I do better and think better when I leave the country. A different atmosphere always does it to me.

I called my uncle, my mum's brother, Michael Salomon. He had been in Oslo, Norway, for over thirty years. I made the international call, and the phone rang.

"Hey, Uncle."

"Who is this?"

"It's me, Linda's son. Your nephew."

"How are you? It's been a while. What's the honor that you're calling?" he said.

"Penny and I are thinking of coming to visit you, to relax, think, and see what Oslo has to offer.

My uncle laughed. "Come on, guys. I'm here. Send me your flight information, and I will pick you guys up."

I hung up feeling good. It was time for a change.

I called my sister, and the phone rang.

"Hey, sis."

"Hey, bro."

"I have the perfect idea."

"You always have an idea. I'm listening," Penny said.

"In the next three weeks, I'm buying us tickets to Oslo, Norway, to see Uncle Michael."

"Why?"

"We need to get away for a while, something different. You're coming."

"Ok, bro; if you're going. I'm going."

For the next two weeks, I got ready to leave the country. I got us the tickets. I told my business partner, Jay, I was traveling to Norway. Since he and I had this indescribable feeling about traveling the world, he understood.

Andeshia and Claudia called so many times, but I ignored them. I needed time to think. Two days before I left the country, I went to see them both individually.

I went to Andeshia's house unannounced and knocked. She opened the door and jumped on me in a bear hug.

"Hey, hun."

"Hey, baby. I was worried. You ignored my calls. Are you okay?"

"Not really. I have been thinking that I need to get away for a few weeks, nothing crazy. I have to go see my uncle in Oslo, Norway.

She was silent, and then she switched. Tears began running down her face.

"You bastard. You piece of shit. You fucking nigga. You're just like the rest of those fucking niggas out there. Now you want to run and leave the fucking country. And I fucking told you I was pregnant. No calls, no nothing, and now you're leaving the country. Fuck off and die, nigga." She went inside and slammed the door so hard it sent shivers down my body.

For the first time in my life, my whole body shut down. I was in shock because I had never seen or heard Andeshia curse or use vulgar language like she just had. It was unbelievably shocking.

I don't know if she was in emotional distress, but in my head, I held Andeshia to such a high standard because she had an educational upbringing and an exceptional caliber of class. She was a ten in all aspects.

I stared at the door for five minutes, wishing she would come back. I knocked a few times, but there was no answer. I left.

I headed to Claudia's house, and in an hour and a half, I got there. I walked toward the door and knocked. I knocked again. There was no answer.

I was walking away when I heard the door open. I turned back around and stared at Claudia. "Come home," I said.

"I'm already home," she said.

"I meant come home to me."

She laughed. She walked to me and kissed me. "You remembered me," she said. "Anyway, I have news for you. I'm pregnant," she said. "I took four pregnancy tests. All of them came back positive. I have them in the house to show you."

I opened my mouth, but no words came out. I wasn't surprised. I'd had a feeling.

"You don't look surprised," she said.

I was quiet. I just followed her into the house.

She showed me all four of the pregnancy tests she had taken. What made it classical was the next statement that came out her mouth. "I have one pregnancy test right now to take in front of you, in case you don't believe me."

Before I opened my mouth to answer, she walked into the bathroom. She left the door open, and she did the whole ordeal in front of me. Then she walked toward me and handed me the pregnancy test.

She looked at me and said, "You are going to be a father."

I looked at her and opened my mouth, but the words didn't come out. I smiled. What a day.

"Hun, I'm leaving the country in two days for a few weeks. I need to clear my head, to think, reason, take care of business, and see my uncle. I will see you when I come back."

"Ok, hun. I will be here when you get back."

She walked to me, stuck her tongue down my throat, and kissed me. I was surprised and mostly impressed. But my recovery was rapid.

"All right, hun; I'm leaving. I need to finish packing."

"Love you; call me. Do you need me to take you the airport?" she said.

"No. It's fine. I will call you, hun." I walked out of her house.

It felt different. The way Claudia had acted was what I had expected from Andeshia. But it was the other way around.

Funny. I went home to finish my packing. I called Andeshia two more times—no answer.

29

The flight from JFK was long. My sister and I arrived at the airport at nine o' clock. Our flight was long, eleven hours nonstop to Oslo. We slept and talked for most of the flight.

Our uncle picked us up and drove us to his place. He was excited to see us.

Norway was breathtaking; it was different. We all had a blast. From the theaters to the restaurants to the people to the cafés. I forgot I had to go back. My sister and I stayed in Oslo for twelve weeks. We had an amazing time; nothing else mattered. I was so relaxed and at peace; it was phenomenal.

Time went by so fast. The next thing I knew, we had to fly back. I was flying back on a Friday to arrive in New York on a Saturday.

On Friday morning, I called Andeshia seven times, but there was no answer. I left messages, but she still didn't call back. I figured she didn't want to talk.

I called Claudia. She answered and was excited to hear from me.

"I have missed you so much," she said. "Please come home. I need to see you. Please come home."

"I fly back today; I arrive tomorrow afternoon. I'll call you once I land."

30

Our flights arrived at JFK at six fifteen on Saturday evening. My uncle was sad we left. But he knew we had to go.

JFK was crowded with so many people that it took us an hour and a half just to clear customs and get our luggage. My sister was tired; we walked out of the airport and hailed a cab.

It took us close to two hours just to get home with traffic and all. We were exhausted.

I walked into my house. I went upstairs, took off my clothes, and took a cold shower. I let the water just run on me with my eyes closed. Back to reality. After the shower, I went to bed and slept like a baby.

I woke up at ten next morning, and my sister brought me breakfast—scrambled eggs, sausages, and bread—and coffee.

"Bro, get up, and eat. What is this? We're back now. We have so much to do."

"I'm up, sis." I got up, went to wash my face, and then came back and ate. I took a shower and got dressed. I had calls to make, people to see, and things to get. I called my business partner, and the phone rang.

"What's happening?"

"I'm back."

"I see that. Come see me; we have things to discuss."

"I will be there in four hours."

"Bye."

"Bye."

I went to Andeshia's house. She wasn't there. It looked like she hadn't been there in a while. I left, and I went to Claudia's house. She was there, as excited as ever.

"Hey, hun."

She was so excited. She started ripping my clothes off.

"Calm down, hun, I have to go see Jay in an hour. I will be back."

"Then we have half an hour to do it."

"You're still pregnant. I'm confused."

"Of course I am. Don't you see my belly? Is there a law that says pregnant woman can't have sex? I'm the one who's confused."

I laughed. "Very funny."

"Come here."

I left there two hours later. I went to Jay's house. He was home. His mum opened the door for me. I bowed and greeted her, "*Como esta?*" I gave her a hug and went to see my friend.

We got down to business, talking and discussing a trip that we had to take. While we were talking, the phone rang.

"That's you or me."

"It's mine." I looked at the phone. My little sister was calling me from overseas.

"Hey, sis."

"Bro, Dad just died."

I collapsed, phone in hand. I was on the floor with tears running down my face. My world shattered. Everything inside me died in that second. "Sis, are you still there?" I could hear she was crying too. "Sis, I will be on the next flight."

I hung up. I called Penny, and the phone rang. "Sis, are you there?"

"Bro, what happened?"

"Chinwe just called. Dad just died."

Penny screamed, and the phone went dead.

My dad had been battling prostate cancer for three years; he had caught it late, and it had gotten into his bones. But death was the last thing anyone expected.

He had been an international business man, and he was doing some business in Africa when he stopped in a hospital for a checkup. And they caught the cancer and told him. They had to run test after test, and it became an ongoing thing. He got admitted.

"Jay, book two tickets for me and my sis. I'm going back home."

I left his house in a cold rage. I had died inside; there was no reason to exist. I was shaken.

I got home in an hour and a half to find my sister balled up in the shower with her clothes on. The shower was running, and tears were streaming down her face like clear diamonds. She was screaming.

I stopped and stared at her for less than a second before joining her, clothes on and everything.

I walked into the shower and held her. She was shaking, and tears were still coming down. We were there for at least an hour before I got up and carried her to her room. I closed the door and left. Every bone inside me was numb.

I went into my room, sat on my bed, wet clothes and all, and passed out.

I woke up shivering at five o'clock in the morning. I got up in a daze, took my clothes off, and put on sweat pants and a tank top.

The next morning, I got up. I woke my sister up and told her we would be leaving in five days.

I called Claudia and told her I was leaving the country again because my dad had died. She wanted to come, to console me and be there. I said no. I needed to be alone.

Five days later, I was at JFK flying out again. This time, it was a sixteen-hour flight.

Everyone was flying in; bad news travels fast. Before I boarded the flight, my mum called. She was in a different state of mind. She said before he died, my dad had held her hand. "He put his hand in his mouth and bit hard. He didn't want to go, but he was slipping away." Tears came down from her eyes. "His eyes closed…" She screamed.

My little sister and little brother, Tobi, were also there with him.

Tears and tears and tears and tears and screaming.

We landed overseas at five o'clock their time. It took us another six hours to get to where the family was. Mum and members of our family were waiting; they came, took our bags, and hugged us.

We went in. So many families and friends from all over the world came by daily to show respect and give their condolences. They offered gifts and money and sympathy. It was a long sad week.

I was the eldest son, so I had to buy the coffin to bury my father. It took me three weeks to find the perfect coffin. I wanted the best. And I found it. The coffin was rose gold with chestnut-wine wood and clear glass inside. It was exceptional.

I hired a car to transport the coffin to the morgue so my dad could be put into it.

The wake was in two days.

On the day of the wake, we all wore white. Just the family—my brothers, sisters, and I.

Two thousand people came. It was a sad day. The priest came to pray. We all had to stand around the coffin. It was open, with the clear glass covering my dad. While the priest prayed, my mum just walked toward the coffin.

"Open the glass."

The priest said, "Ma'am, what are you doing?"

"Don't you dare talk to me or question me when I'm talking to my husband."

Everybody's mouths dropped open. My mum opened the glass, picked my dad's head up, and kissed him for a good four minutes and thirty-five seconds. She said, "Darling, why did you leave me?"

There was complete silence. No one spoke. Mind you, my dad had been dead for over twelve weeks at that point.

I stared at my mum, and a tear came to my eye. And I knew that I wanted a woman to love me like that for the rest of my life, to kiss me and talk to me twelve weeks after I'm dead, when I'm about to go six feet under.

She defined what true love was and what a woman was supposed to be.

The End

www.ingramcontent.com/pod-product-compliance
Lightning Source LLC
Chambersburg PA
CBHW030937090426
42737CB00007B/467
9780692552674